Learning to Use the BBC Microcomputer

Learning to Use the BBC Microcomputer
by P. N. Dane

Gower
A Read-Out Publication

© P. N. Dane, 1982

Reprinted 1983

All rights reserved. No part of this publication may be reproduced, stored in a retrieval system, or transmitted in any form or by any means, electronic, mechanical, photocopying, recording, or otherwise, without the prior permission of Gower Publishing Company Limited.

Published by
Gower Publishing Company Limited,
Gower House, Croft Road, Aldershot,
Hampshire GU11 3HR, England

British Library Cataloguing in Publication Data

Dane, P. N.
   Learning to Use the BBC Microcomputer
   1. BBC (Computer)
   I. Title
   001.64'04   QA76.8.B/
   ISBN 0-566-03452-2

Printed and bound in England
by FD Graphics, Fleet, Hampshire

Contents

List of Figures — vii
Foreword — ix

Chapter 1. Introduction to the BBC Microcomputer — 1
What is the BBC Microcomputer? — 1
How was the BBC Microcomputer developed? — 3
What can the BBC Microcomputer do? — 5
How can the BBC Microcomputer be extended? — 7
What are some typical applications of the BBC Microcomputer? — 9
Summary — 12

Chapter 2. Using the BBC Microcomputer — 13
Switching on — 13
The screen — 14
The keyboard — 14
Loading a program — 16
Editing — 18
Giving simple instructions to the BBC Microcomputer — 19
The BBC Microcomputer as a calculator — 22
Summary — 23
Self-test questions — 24

Chapter 3. Introduction to programming — 25
Writing and running simple programs — 25
Giving data to a program while it is running — 28
Making decisions in programs — 30
Repetition in programs — 34
More programs — 35
Saving programs — 39
Using the printer — 41
Summary — 41
Self-test questions — 42

Chapter 4. Coloured writing and graphics — 45
Coloured writing — 45
Coloured pictures — 47
The screen and memory — 48

v

Putting a character on the screen — 50
Producing a drawing — 51
The screen co-ordinates — 53
Writing anywhere on the screen — 54
Screen patterns and colour — 55
User-controlled movement — 57
Animation — 59
Dynamic simulation — 60
Drawing lines on the screen — 61
Summary — 64

Chapter 5. Special features of the BBC Microcomputer — 65
Specification of the BBC Microcomputer — 65
Inside the BBC Microcomputer — 67
Special features — 69
    The BBC Microcomputer's clock — 69
    Available storage — 70
    Examining the contents of a location — 71
How the BBC Microcomputer stores a program — 71
General utilisation of memory — 74
Sound on the BBC Microcomputer — 74

Conclusions — 76

Appendix 1   Further reading — 79
Appendix 2   Glossary — 80

List of Figures

1.1	The BBC Microcomputer	1
1.2	Inside the BBC Microcomputer	2
1.3	An example of the graphics produced by the BBC Microcomputer	3
1.4	A cassette and a floppy disk	6
1.5	A cassette unit attached to the BBC Microcomputer	6
1.6	A printer attached to the BBC Microcomputer	7
1.7	Back view of the BBC Microcomputer, showing connection points and the ON/OFF switch	8
1.8	Underneath of the BBC Microcomputer	9
1.9	Robot arm	9
1.10	Graph plotter	10
2.1	Screen display when the BBC Microcomputer is switched on	13
2.2	Dialogue after loading a program from cassette	17
2.3	Dialogue after the command LOAD "SKETCH"	17
2.4	A string stored in memory	20
2.5	Numbers stored in the memory after A = 3: B = 4	23
3.1	The results of running a program	26
3.2	Flow chart for simple maths drill program	31
3.3	Flow chart for improved maths drill program	33
3.4	Two parallel arrays for translation program	38
3.5	Dialogue after saving a program	40
4.1	Memory map for the BBC Microcomputer screen	49
4.2	Table of the teletext graphics characters and their codes	50
4.3	(a) Butterfly. (b) Butterfly with grid. (c) Butterfly composed of graphics characters. (d) Outline of image plotted on screen	51
4.4	Butterfly as displayed on the screen	53
4.5	Control keys and directions	58
4.6	Frames 1, 2 and 3 for flying Butterfly	61
4.7	Flow chart for mobile display program	61
5.1	Inside view of the BBC Microcomputer	69
5.2	How a BASIC program is stored	72
5.3	Storage of a short BASIC program	73
5.4	General memory utilisation in the BBC Microcomputer	74

Foreword

The BBC Microcomputer was specially designed and built to be launched on the market at the same time as the popular BBC television series on Computer Literacy. The microcomputer represented an entirely new generation of home computers because it included an unusually wide and exciting range of facilities and features. These make it suitable for almost any purpose. The BBC Microcomputer is expected to herald the start of a new era in public awareness of computers — and, in my opinion, certainly deserves to do so!

Many people will buy the BBC Microcomputer as their first introduction to computing. They will therefore need a book which introduces the ideas of computing — with particular reference to the BBC Microcomputer — in a straightforward and simple fashion. This book sets out to provide this. It gives down-to-earth and jargon-free information about the BBC Microcomputer; it explains how to use the BBC Microcomputer and its very wide range of facilities; it describes many applications of the BBC Microcomputer, including those for business, education and hobbies, and it also gives a simple and direct introduction to programming the BBC Microcomputer in BASIC, the language which is used to control it. Much acknowledgement is due to Garry Marshall, whose book on *Learning to use the PET Computer* provided a model for this book.

In particular the BBC Microcomputer is renowned for the way that it can produce coloured displays and sound. This book pays particular attention to these: it describes how to produce pictures and diagrams, both in colour as well as black and white, and it presents programs for a large number of graphics applications. It also describes ways of generating music. These will almost certainly stimulate the reader to further investigation of the facilities and applications of the BBC Microcomputer.

My own interest in computers goes back to the time, many years ago, when I was taken for a tour inside one of the old valve-based, main-frame computers. In those days people could actually walk between the racks of glowing valves that constituted the memory inside the computer itself! However, my real excitement over computers only began with the arrival of microcomputers. These, being at a price that people could afford, brought computing into the home. I have experience with a wide range of them, but must admit to an especially great excitement for the BBC Microcomputer which I was lucky enough to have been able to use from the summer of 1981 when early production models first became available. The more I have used the BBC Microcomputer, the more the excitement has grown. The BBC Microcomputer really does open up a new dimension in microcomputing. Not only are its facilities as good as everyone says they are; they are easy to program too!

Just as I was excited and enthusiastic when I first got my hands on the BBC Microcomputer, I see the same sort of reactions in other people when this happens to them. I am sure that readers of this book will feel exactly the same way. But, having got their hands on a BBC Microcomputer, the immediate problem will be how to use it. This book should help.

P.N.D.

Chapter 1
Introduction to the BBC Microcomputer

What is the BBC Microcomputer?

The BBC Microcomputer belongs to a group of computers called microcomputers, or micros. They are given this name for several reasons. Firstly they are extremely small compared with early computers; secondly they are also small compared with industrial computers (or main-frames); and lastly they have microprocessors as their electronic 'hearts'.

As you can see from Figure 1.1, the BBC Microcomputer consists of a case containing a keyboard, rather like that of a conventional typewriter. In use, the BBC Microcomputer requires a screen of some sort for its display, but to keep down costs, it has been designed to work with an ordinary television set. Inside the BBC Microcomputer, as is shown in Figure 1.2, there are a number of integrated circuits. One is the microprocessor, and the others provide the BBC Microcomputer's memory and can store information — but there is no need for you to worry

Figure 1.1 The BBC Microcomputer.

1

about them. Although the electronic circuitry and devices are fascinating, you do not need to understand them in order to be able to use the BBC Microcomputer — and this introductory book is about using the BBC Microcomputer.

The keyboard is for communicating with the computer. Commands for it to obey and information for it to store can simply be typed in. Because the keyboard is set out in the same way as that of a typewriter, a trained typist can type on it as quickly, if not more so, than on a typewriter. Right at the outset of using the computer, you may like to try proper typing techniques rather than just single-finger typing, because this will save tremendous amounts of time in the long run. Anything you type on the keyboard automatically appears on the screen used for the display.

The BBC Microcomputer possesses a number of what are called 'screen editing facilities'. These make it simple and easy for you to 'edit' your typing, i.e. to correct errors, to make changes, and to arrange for the revised typing to appear on the screen. The BBC Microcomputer's screen editing facilities have been very carefully thought out. With a little practice, you will find them easy to use.

Besides letting you produce displays of letters and numbers, the BBC Microcomputer also lets you draw simple pictures on the screen. This

Figure 1.2   Inside the BBC Microcomputer.

2

facility is known as 'graphics'. The BBC Microcomputer is particularly renowned for its graphics. Figure 1.3 illustrates the sort of graphics display that the BBC Microcomputer can produce. The BBC Microcomputer's impressive graphics are a tremendous bonus, because the imaginative use of pictures, diagrams and graphs livens up the presentation of information. Applications are widespread, for example for computer games, in education and in business.

The BBC Microcomputer is light and compact, and is small enough to be carried from room to room, or even from house to house, where it can be set up quickly and easily. It only requires to be plugged into the mains supply and connected to an ordinary domestic television. Furthermore, as soon as it is switched on, it is ready to accept instructions, provided you give them in a language that it can understand. This language is BASIC, and it enables you to issue commands which are promptly and automatically obeyed by the BBC Microcomputer.

How was the BBC Microcomputer developed?

The event that signalled the advent of microelectronics, and hence of microcomputers, was the space race of the 1960s between the USA and

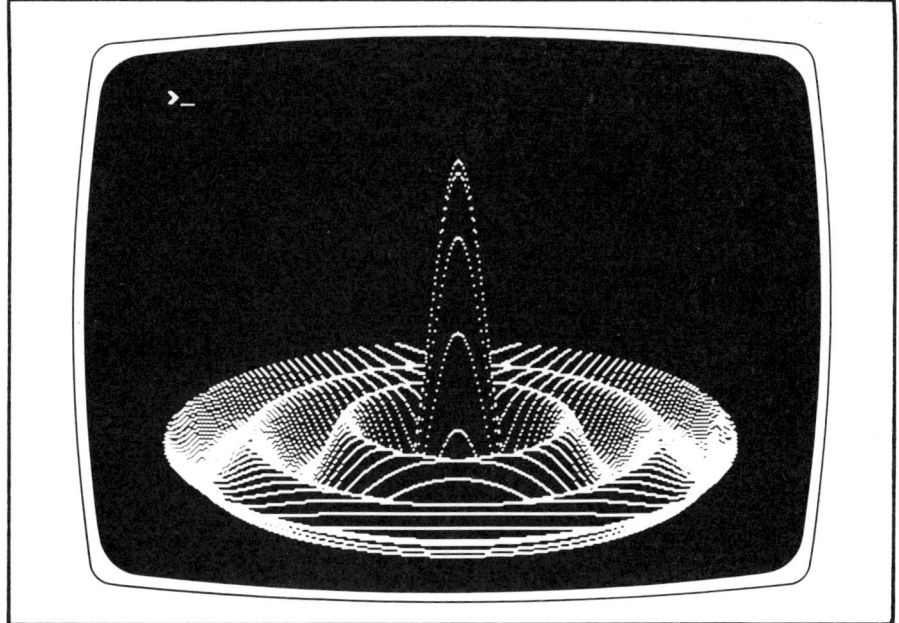

Figure 1.3 An example of the graphics produced by the BBC Microcomputer.

3

Russia. Because American rockets were less powerful than those of the Russians, the Americans needed to reduce the weight, and hence the size of everything that had to be carried by their rockets — including all the electronics. This stimulated the American electronics industry to investigate and develop means of miniaturising their electronic circuitry. The developments culminated in the microprocessor, which in addition to being extremely small, considering its capabilities, is a multi-purpose device in the sense that it can perform any electronic function for which it can be programmed. This versatility has led to the use of microprocessors in a tremendous number of applications. The consequent mass production of microprocessors has caused the cost per unit to drop to a matter of a few pence. The BBC Microcomputer is based on the 6502 microprocessor. It is manufactured by Acorn of Cambridge under licence from the BBC and the Government (in the form of the Department of Industry). The BBC Microcomputer achieves some of its special functions by using special logic arrays manufactured in Britain by Ferranti.

The microprocessor in the BBC Microcomputer is the same as that used in many of the amusement arcade games, such as 'space invaders'. Ironically, given the military origins of microelectronics, these microprocessors are more advanced examples of the technology than those used in the guidance systems of inter-continental ballistic missiles!

Although the core of the BBC Microcomputer is a microprocessor — and this does all the hard work, all the computing, you can tap its potential without having any knowledge at all of how it works.

Throughout 1981 the computing world was agog with interest at the announcements that the BBC was to commission a microcomputer in connection with its television series on Computer Literacy. The BBC Microcomputer itself became available early in 1982. It was awaited with considerable excitement and interest because its facilities were a marked improvement on those of any other microcomputer in the same price range. Although dozens of new microcomputers come on to the market every year, each one normally representing a slight technical advance, it is rare for a microcomputer to take such a leap forward in setting new standards. No doubt other manufacturers will try to follow its lead, but it may be some time before there is another computer with facilities to match those of the BBC Microcomputer at a similar price.

There are two models of the BBC Microcomputer, namely Model A and Model B. The most obvious difference between them is in terms of what is called 'user-programmable memory': any program that is to be run on a computer requires a certain amount of memory in which to store it. The more memory that the computer possesses, then the wider will be the length and range of programs that it can store and run. The screen display uses part of this same memory. The more complex the screen display, then the more memory it will take up. The greater the memory taken up for the screen display, then the less is available for storing and running programs. Some programs require more memory than others. In particular, a great deal of memory is required by some business programs, wordprocessing programs and even games programs. This type of memory is known as 'user-programmable memory' because it is used in connection with the user's own programs. Memory is measured in terms of what are called 'kilobytes' — represented by K — and this is discussed further in the next chapter. For the present purpose of distinguishing between the two models of the BBC Microcomputer:

Model A provides 16K of user-programmable memory, whereas

Model B provides 32K of user-programmable memory.

Model B is almost certainly necessary for sophisticated business packages, but Model A may be adequate for simple programming and for running games programs.

What can the BBC Microcomputer do?

Fundamentally, a BBC Microcomputer can do anything that you can tell it to do, which is to say that it will obey any instruction or set of instructions that it is given. A set of instructions to a computer is usually called a computer program. So the BBC Microcomputer, like any other computer, executes programs and does what you tell it to do. Thus one way to make use of a BBC Microcomputer is to learn to program it in its own language. Its natural language is BASIC. This is a simple programming language that is designed to be easy both to learn and to use. Incidentally, although BASIC is the natural language of the BBC Microcomputer, it is not the natural language of the microprocessor. So BASIC has to be translated into the code understood by the microprocessor, which is known as its 'machine code' — but this second level of translation happens automatically and you will be unaware of it when you are using the computer. It is also possible to program the BBC Microcomputer directly in its machine code, but this book will not go into how. Machine code programs are considerably more difficult to write, although they do give programs which run at greater speed because there is no time taken up in the translation between BASIC and machine code.

However it is not essential to be an expert programmer to use the BBC Microcomputer since some programs are supplied with the machine when it is purchased. These programs come on a cassette tape called the

'Welcome tape'. Many programs are already available for the BBC Microcomputer and you may like to have a look at the hobby computer magazines for their advertisements. A much wider range will soon be available. Many commercial firms will be supplying programs specially for the BBC Microcomputer, and many are already advertised in the press. They will be available on cassette tapes — which are of the same type as good quality audio cassettes — or on what are known as 'floppy disks'. Figure 1.4 shows a cassette and a floppy disk. To transfer a program from

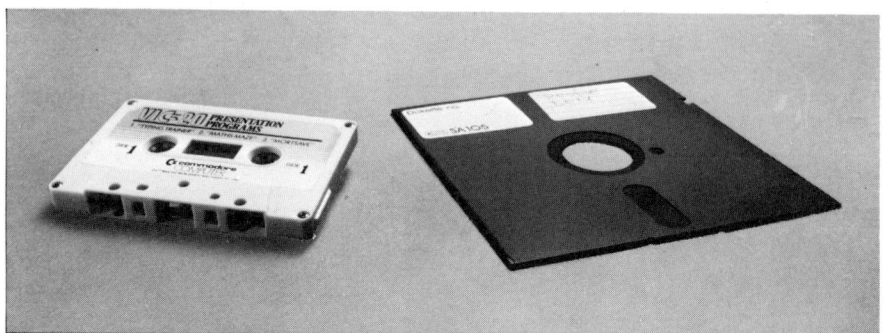

Figure 1.4 A cassette and a floppy disk.

Figure 1.5 A cassette unit attached to the BBC Microcomputer.

either a cassette tape or a floppy disk to the BBC Microcomputer requires either a cassette tape system (player/recorder) or a disk unit. Figure 1.5 shows a cassette tape recorder attached to the BBC Microcomputer. Programs available on disk or cassette tape are known as 'software'. This is in contrast with 'hardware' which is part — or parts — of the computer itself.

The BBC Microcomputer can do a lot of things. Like with most other microcomputers, you can often make it do these things without, yourself, having any knowledge of how to program it. Nevertheless it is often useful to be able to program, if only to amend or modify an existing program. Besides, programming is fun! It is easy to do and it provides a means of expressing and communicating your own ideas to the computer, so that it can test them for you.

How can the BBC Microcomputer be extended?

Besides performing computations and storing information, the BBC Microcomputer can, again like any other computer, be used in conjunction with other devices. Units which can be connected to it, and controlled by it, are called 'peripherals'. You met two of them in the previous section: the cassette and the floppy disk. These are peripherals used for permanent storage of information by means of a magnetic pattern — either on the tape or the disk. Other peripherals include temperature sensors, computer operated switches for turning on and off external

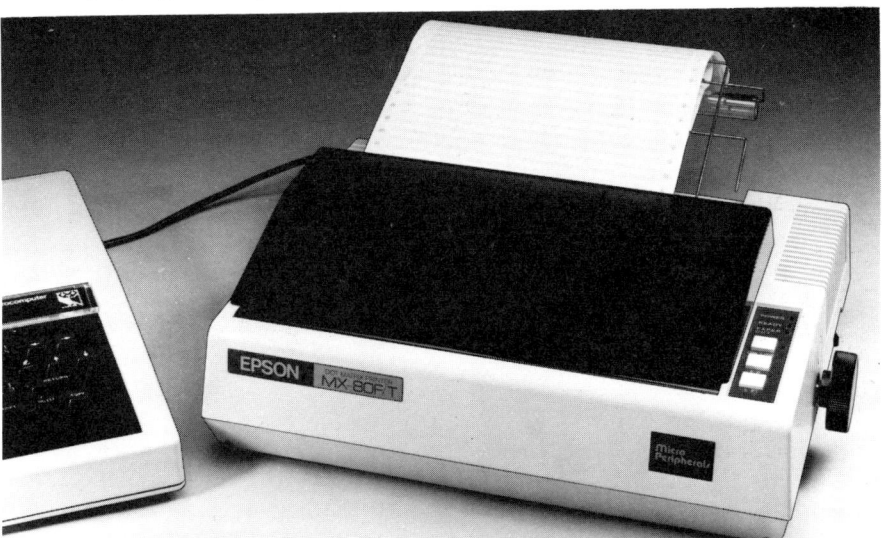

Figure 1.6 A printer attached to the BBC Microcomputer.

7

electrical devices and even robot modules.

For many computer applications it is useful to have the results of the computer's work in written form to provide a permanent record of the results of computations. This printed output is called a 'printout'. A printer is an essential peripheral for producing printouts. It can be attached to the BBC Microcomputer as shown in Figure 1.6.

Some peripherals are connected to the BBC Microcomputer using the connections at the back. For Model B further peripherals are attached via the connectors underneath. Figure 1.7 shows the back view of the BBC Microcomputer with its connection sockets for peripherals. The actual connections depend on the model and the types of peripherals. These can include: UHF television output, two separate video outputs, a serial output for a printer, the connector for a cassette tape recorder, an analogue connector for games paddles and an econet connector for joining several BBC Microcomputers together.

There is a 'user-port' on a socket underneath Model B. A port is a connection between the computer and the outside world — just as an airport or boat port connects a place with the outside world. A port is described as a user-port when signals there can be controlled by the program written by the user. They can, for example, be used to communicate with another device, turn heating on or off or even control a robot. Printers that require a parallel port and disk units are usually attached to the sockets underneath the Model B of the BBC Microcomputer (see Figure 1.8).

Many other devices can be added to the BBC Microcomputer via these connections. The applications that are outwardly most impressive to many people are those that involve the control of mechanical devices. One example is the robot arm as seen in the BBC TV Computer Literacy series. It is shown in Figure 1.9. A second example is a graph plotter which is shown in Figure 1.10. Under the control of the BBC Microcomputer, it can produce high quality drawings.

These examples cover only a few of the devices that can be used to extend the BBC Microcomputer, but they should be sufficient to show

Figure 1.7 Back view of the BBC Microcomputer, showing connection points and the ON/OFF switch.

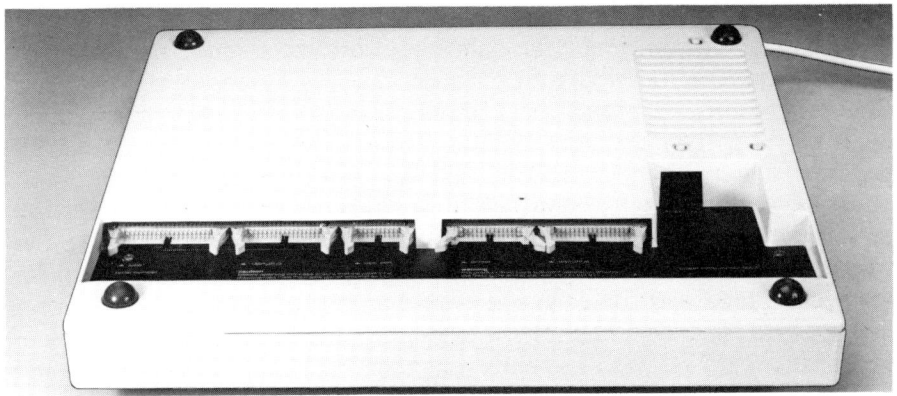

Figure 1.8 Underneath of the BBC Microcomputer.

that the BBC Microcomputer can open up a wide range of interests and activities.

What are some typical applications of the BBC Microcomputer?

The BBC Microcomputer was designed with many serious applications in

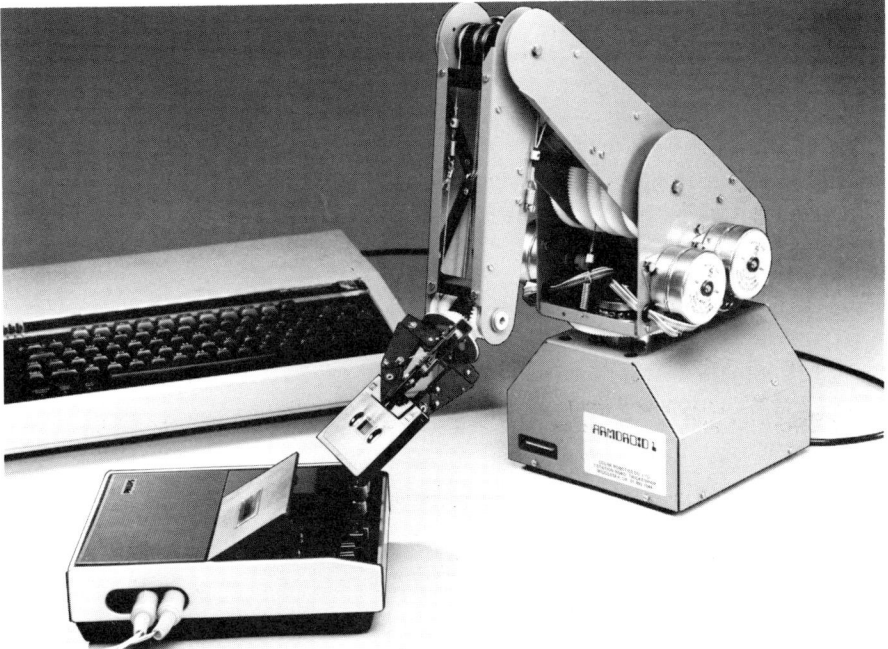

Figure 1.9 Robot arm.

9

mind. The areas in which it can be used can be broadly classified as: in the home for personal and recreational use; in educational institutions and in business.

For personal use there are games programs of many kinds, as illustrated on the Welcome tape. Using the BBC Microcomputer for playing games could be criticised as a frivolous use of a personal computer, and there is no doubt that many games are lighthearted. Nevertheless they do serve a useful purpose for relaxation and entertainment. On the other hand, there are many imaginative games which have educational value. They can teach or help to develop attributes ranging over simple manipulation and co-ordination skills in children, the mental disciplines required to find solution methods for puzzles, and testing strategies and tactics against situations presented by the computer. There are many chess-playing programs of a formidable standard. Although they are, at the moment, only available for other microcomputers, they will shortly be available for the BBC Microcomputer too.

The presence of a BBC Microcomputer in the home means that educational activities need not be restricted to schools and colleges. Computer assisted learning packages have been available for some time on other computers and are being converted for use on the BBC

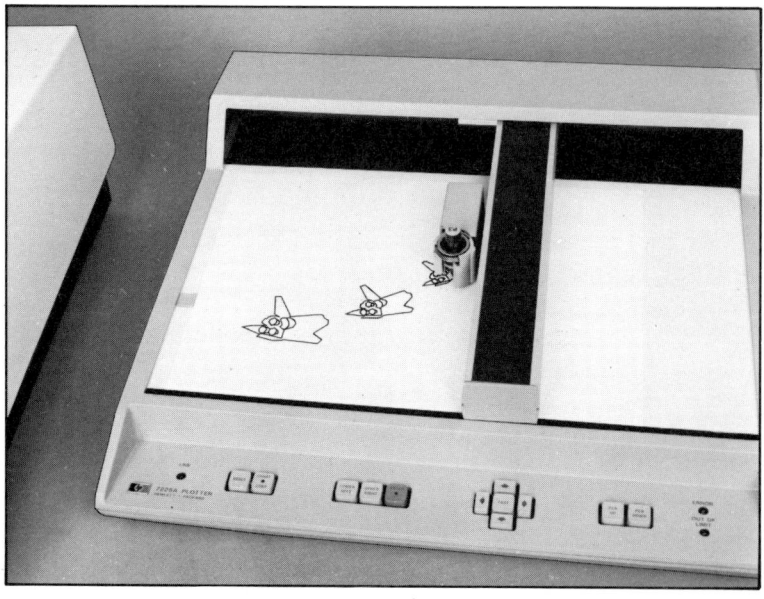

Figure 1.10 Graph plotter.

10

Microcomputer. These can be used just as effectively at home as at school. Computer assisted learning is not, in any case, intended to replace teachers, but to assist them by providing another educational tool. In a post-industrial society it is important to expose everyone, particularly children, to the current technology so that they may be aware of it, appreciate its capabilities and thus be in a position to take advantage of it and so develop it in some way. The presence of a BBC Microcomputer as an everyday item in the home or at school can help to achieve this objective.

In schools microcomputers have many valid uses ranging over computer assisted learning, instructional programs, and the use of quiz programs. In higher education the BBC Microcomputer is ideal for activities such as undergraduate project work: programming projects can be carried out on it, as well as electronics projects, using the BBC Microcomputer to control or monitor electronic equipment attached to it.

As a business aid, the BBC Microcomputer may appear in a number of different guises. It will almost certainly have a disk unit attached to it and may have a second processor and more memory attached as well. For any activity where large amounts of information have to be stored and certain items have to be retrieved, it is almost essential to use a disk rather than a cassette unit for storage. This is not only because a disk has a greater storage capacity, but also because it permits an item of information to be got out of storage or 'accessed' much more rapidly. Any item stored on the disk can be accessed almost at once regardless of its position. By contrast, with a cassette tape it is necessary to wind the tape on as far as the required item before accessing it. This can mean long delays, which can be very irritating if you are doing much accessing.

Serious professional users will probably want an operating system called CP/M. Under this operating system a very large amount of software, written over the years, will be available for immediate use on the BBC Microcomputer. CP/M will operate the BBC Microcomputer if it has its memory expanded with a second processor and is used with a disk system.

Adapters are planned for the BBC Microcomputer to allow it to act as an intelligent terminal attached to the Prestel computer information system, available over the telephone. This will allow the user to access Prestel's vast amount of information, to book theatre tickets, book holidays, pay bills, and much more. All this from the convenience of the arm-chair at home!

All these activities can be performed using existing programs. However, if you learn to program the BBC Microcomputer, you can write your own programs. Not only can these express your own ideas, but also, as in most spheres, what you can buy seldom does exactly what you would like it to do. Since the BBC Microcomputer is much faster at numerical calculations than mere people, it would seem sensible to get the BBC Microcomputer to do any calculations that you require. Besides acting as a source of entertainment, and educational and business convenience, the BBC Microcomputer can, in the information age, be used to extend and amplify the human brain.

Summary

The BBC Microcomputer is a small microcomputer which comes in two versions: Model A and Model B. Model B has the greater capabilities because it has the greater memory and may be expanded for use with a disk system.

The major novelty of a microcomputer is its size rather than its ability to compute. However, the smallness of a microcomputer is what makes computing power available for use as personal tools in the home or at work. This smallness is a direct result of recent technological developments.

The BBC Microcomputer can be used in many ways, but its main areas of application seem to be in business, education and for personal entertainment. Computer programs can be bought to perform many tasks in these areas. This allows the BBC Microcomputer to be usefully employed as soon as it is acquired without any expertise in programming being necessary. Clearly, as time progresses, more and more programs will become available for the BBC Microcomputer.

The capabilities of the BBC Microcomputer can be extended in a variety of ways, either by adding extras to the computer itself or by acquiring further units or peripherals, such as a printer, which can be attached to the BBC Microcomputer and used in conjunction with it.

Chapter 2
Using the BBC Microcomputer

Switching on

To turn on the BBC Microcomputer, plug it into the mains in the usual way and turn it on. (The position of its on/off switch is shown in Figure 1.7). Almost immediately a display such as that shown in Figure 2.1 appears on the screen. The top line of the display means that the BBC Microcomputer is ready to accept and display instructions given to it in its BASIC language.

The second line reveals how much of the BBC Microcomputer's memory is available to the user. As mentioned in the previous chapter, this memory is measured in *kilobytes*. A byte is a single storage location. You will remember that Model B of the BBC Microcomputer has 32 kilobytes of memory. Surprising as it may seem, a kilobyte does not equal

Figure 2.1 Screen display when the BBC Microcomputer is switched on.

13

a thousand bytes, as you may imagine if you are familiar with the metric system. Because powers of 2 are always useful numbers in computer systems, 1K actually equals 2 raised to the power 10, i.e. 1024:

32K − 32 − 1024 = 32768 bytes or storage locations

So the memory of Model B of the BBC Microcomputer is 32768 bytes (or storage locations). However, about 3580 of these are required as a sort of note book for the BBC Microcomputer to use while running a BASIC program, and at least one kilobyte will be used by the screen display memory. So for Model B the amount of memory that is free for use is:

32768 − 3580 − 1025 = 28163 bytes (storage locations)

A similar short calculation gives the storage available on Model A of the BBC Microcomputer. You may like to try it for yourself.

The third line of the display shows a symbol like this > and a flashing dash, which is called a 'cursor'. Together these indicate that the BBC Microcomputer is ready for use. Whatever you type on the keyboard will appear on the screen at the position of the flashing cursor, and the cursor will move on as you type.

The screen

The letters, symbols and numbers that you can type from the keyboard are all called 'characters'. The screen is wide enough to take 40 characters on a line. Once the line is full up with the 40 characters, the cursor automatically moves to the beginning of the next line. This is where the next character appears.

The screen can hold 25 lines, each of 40 characters. So a character can be placed in any of 25 by 40 (= 1000) positions on the screen. When the bottom line of the screen has been filled, the screen contents automatically shift up by one line giving a new blank bottom line. This is called 'scrolling upwards'. The previous top line disappears.

The keyboard

The keyboard characters consist of letters, numbers and symbols. There is also a space-bar which produces the spaces between the words. Using the keyboard is just like using an ordinary typewriter. However there are a number of special features which this section will explain.

Firstly, on the bottom left-hand side of the keyboard, you will notice three lights under the headings 'cassette motor', 'caps lock' and 'shift lock'. When the BBC Microcomputer is first turned on, the light under the caps-lock heading will glow. This indicates that all letters that you type from the keyboard will come out in capitals, i.e. upper-case. If you touch the key labelled CAPS LOCK once, the caps-lock light goes out. Touch it again and the caps-lock light comes back on again. While the caps-lock light is on, all letters that you type will be in capitals. While the caps-lock light is off, all letters that you type will be in non-capitals, i.e. lower-case. This CAPS LOCK key has no effect at all on typing numbers and symbols such as + and : .

Touching the SHIFT LOCK key turns the shift-lock light first on and then off. While the shift-lock light is on, all letters will be in capitals, just as with an active caps-lock. The difference is with the keys labelled with both numbers and symbols. With an active shift-lock, it is the symbols that appear on the screen rather than the numbers. In computing you will find that you use capital letters more often than lower-case letters and numbers more often than symbols. So it is normally much more useful to work with an active caps-lock. This is why the BBC Microcomputer has been designed so that this is the active mode when the computer is first turned on.

There are three keys which deserve particular attention. They are the RETURN key, the ESCAPE key and the BREAK key.

The RETURN key is on the right-hand side of the keyboard. You use it to tell the computer that you are satisfied with what you have typed and that you want the computer to do something with it. Pressing the RETURN key is known as 'entering'. So pressing the RETURN key enters what you have typed into the computer and requires the computer to take some action as a result. For example, if you have just typed an instruction, pressing the RETURN key to enter it, instructs the computer to obey that instruction.

The ESCAPE key is on the top left-hand side of the keyboard. You can use it if, for any reason, you want to stop the computer while it is working, for example in the middle of a program. This may sound a strange thing to want to do, but in practice you will find that you will need to use it. The ESCAPE key will stop the computer when it is searching through a tape for a program. This can be quite useful if, for example, you discover that the program you want is listed on the screen but not loaded — perhaps because the name you asked the computer to load was typed incorrectly.

The BREAK key is at the top right-hand side of the keyboard. It will do a similar job to the ESCAPE key but using it has its problems: it is possible to wipe out the program from memory if a number is typed immediately after pressing it! If you haven't wiped your program out, it is possible for you to recover, but it is better to get into the habit of using the ESCAPE key rather than the BREAK key.

Loading a program

Probably the most enjoyable and painless way to become familiar with the BBC Microcomputer and its keyboard is to use them to play a game that requires responses from the keyboard. Some of the games on the Welcome tape are ideal for this.

To load any program — irrespective of its name — from a cassette, connect a cassette unit to the BBC Microcomputer and insert the cassette. Completely rewind the cassette and press the 'stop' key on the cassette unit. Next type:

LOAD " "

Then press the RETURN key to signal the computer to act on your instruction. This generates the following message on the screen:

```
Searching
```

Now set the cassette recorder to 'play'. The following messages appear on the screen in succession, where INDEX is the name of the program:

```
Searching
Loading
INDEX     00
>_
```

The final reappearance of the cursor indicates that the BBC Microcomputer has copied the first program on the cassette into its memory. You can run the program merely be typing RUN and entering it by pressing the RETURN key. (If you have loaded a games program, the program itself should now give instructions on how to play the game.)

A set of messages between the computer and the user is called a 'dialogue'. The complete dialogue for the loading procedure is shown in Figure 2.2. This loading procedure always causes the first program on the tape to be copied into the BBC Microcomputer's memory. If you want some later program, you can include its name in the LOAD instruction. Thus to load a program named 'SKETCH' from a cassette, type:

LOAD "SKETCH"

Then enter it by pressing the RETURN key. Figure 2.3 shows the resulting dialogue to the point where the program is copied into the BBC

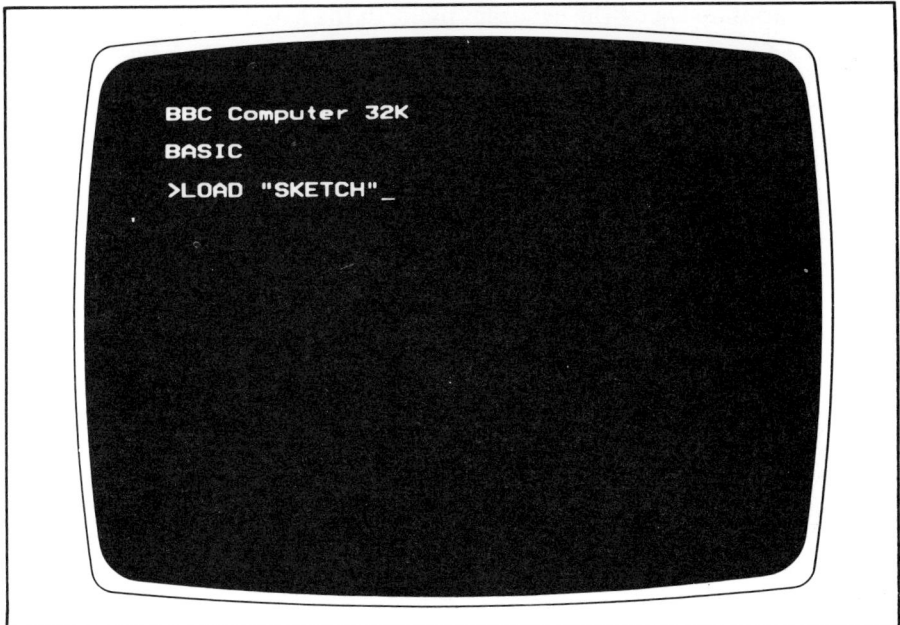

Figure 2.2 Dialogue after loading a program from cassette.

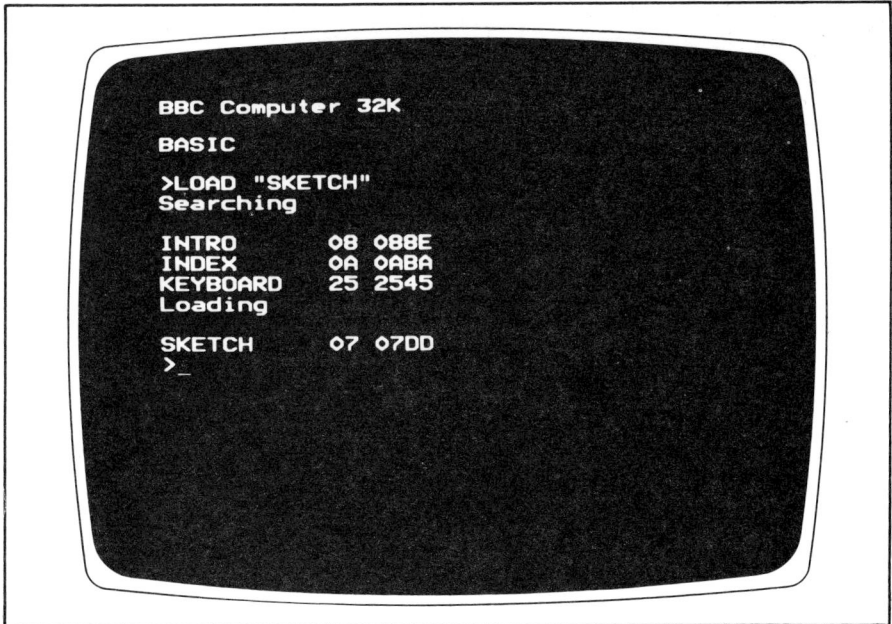

Figure 2.3 Dialogue after the command LOAD "SKETCH".

Microcomputer. Using the program name in the loading instruction saves time, because the computer can ignore other programs which appear before it on the tape. If you ask for a program that does not exist, or if you have typed its name wrongly, you have to wait a long time while the computer searches fruitlessly. You will, however, get printed on the screen a list of the names of the programs that the computer encounters on the tape while it is searching. To avoid long waits, it is sensible to have programs recorded on short C12 cassettes with perhaps only one program, or certainly not more than two, on each side.

Editing

'Editing' is the name given to correcting or altering a piece of typing. The BBC Microcomputer has very good editing facilities. If you realise that you have made a typing mistake immediately you have made it, the simplest way to put it right is by using the DELETE key which is on the bottom right-hand side of the keyboard. Pressing it once makes the cursor go back a space, while at the same time rubbing a character out. Then you can start retyping.

If you have already entered the line of typing with the mistake in it, you will have to re-enter the line correctly. For this there is another method of editing which corrects the mistake without losing the typing. To use this method, you need the four keys that can move the position of the cursor around the screen. These keys have arrows on them pointing left, right, up and down, and they are called the CURSOR-CONTROL keys. They are at the top right-hand corner of the keyboard. You will also need the COPY key which is at the bottom right-hand side of the keyboard. Every time you press it, the character under which the cursor was flashing gets copied to a new line at the bottom of the screen.

Suppose that you want to edit a line of typing which has a wrong character somewhere in the middle. Begin by using the CURSOR-CONTROL keys to place the flashing cursor at the beginning of the line that you want to edit. Then touch the COPY key to copy this first character on to the new line at the bottom of the screen. Then do the same thing for the next letter. When you come to the character that you want changed, press the correct keyboard key instead of the COPY key. This character will be typed on to the new line at the bottom of the screen.

Essentially the new line is constructed from any of the characters you wish to copy from your original line, together with the new characters from any of the other keys you touch on the keyboard. An example will help illustrate this. Suppose you had the following mistyped line on the screen:

WHAT APEARS TO BE THE MATTHER?

You clearly need to add an extra P in APEARS and remove an H from MATTHER. To do this, you will construct a new line with the correct spelling. Position the cursor at the beginning of the line and press the COPY key until you have the following new version:

WHAT AP

At this stage you need to insert another P. So merely touch the letter P on the keyboard once. This will produce the following:

WHAT APP

Now copy in the rest of the line up to MATT, using the COPY key to produce:

WHAT APPEARS TO BE THE MATT

Here there is an H, which you do not want, in the line you are copying. Use the CURSOR-CONTROL key to skip the H by moving the cursor beyond it. Then press the COPY key to copy down the rest of the line as you want it. The result reads:

WHAT APPEARS TO BE THE MATTER?

Such easy screen editing will be a boon to people who are one-finger typists. It will normally be much easier to move the cursor to somewhere on the screen where there are the appropriate letters to copy, rather than to type them out on the keyboard again separately.

Giving simple instructions to the BBC Microcomputer

You can give the BBC Microcomputer instructions which it can act on at once. Like all instructions, they have to be written in the BASIC language. You have already met a few of them, including LOAD and RUN. This section introduces you to some more.

Generally speaking, what a computer does in most situations is to accept and store information of some kind, manipulate or process it, and then give the results in some appropriate form. This can be illustrated by instructing the computer to do something with a set of characters. Such a set of characters is called a 'string'. In the BASIC language the dollar sign $ is used to tell the computer that you want it to treat something as a string. For example the string of characters "NICHOLAS and JONATHAN"

19

can be stored in the BBC Microcomputer's memory by typing and entering the following on a new line:

A$ = "NICHOLAS and JONATHAN"

You will of course remember that you have to press the RETURN key to enter. Pressing RETURN causes the computer to execute this instruction, which it does by giving the name A$ to a part of its memory in which it then stores the string of characters between the inverted commas. This is illustrated in Figure 2.4. This BASIC instruction is equivalent to the plain English instruction: 'store the string of characters between the inverted commas in a part of the memory and give it the name A$'. Note that spaces count as characters just as letters do.

When this instruction is executed, there is no outward sign that anything has happened. To demonstrate that the instruction has been obeyed, you need to know how to get at the information that has just been stored. You can print out the information stored in the part of the memory given the name A$, by typing and entering:

PRINT A$

In response the computer then prints on the screen:

NICHOLAS and JONATHAN

This BASIC instruction can be understood as 'print out what is stored in A$'.

You can instruct the BBC Microcomputer to find the number of characters stored in A$ with the LEN instruction where LEN stands for 'length'. For example suppose you type:

PRINT LEN(A$)

When you press RETURN to enter, the number 21 appears on the screen.

Memory   A$

NICHOLAS AND JONATHAN

Figure 2.4 A string stored in memory.

In this case the 21 characters consist of 19 letters and two spaces. This instruction can be interpreted as 'print out the length of the string stored in A$' or as 'print out the number of characters stored in the string A$'.

BASIC has some features which enable you to manipulate strings. The LEFT$ enables you to pick off a number of characters from the left of the string. RIGHT$ enables you to pick off a number of characters from the right of the string. For example typing and entering:

PRINT LEFT$(A$,8)

causes the computer to print the following eight characters from the left of the string:

NICHOLAS

Typing and entering:

PRINT RIGHT$(A$,8)

gives the following eight characters from the right of the string:

JONATHAN

So the last instruction means 'print the eight characters at the right of the string of characters stored in A$'.

You will realise by now that BASIC instructions are a sort of shorthand for instructions expressed in English. However, because they are a shorthand, they must be expressed in precisely the correct way. If there is a slight error in the way that an instruction is written, no computer will be able to recognise it. The BBC Microcomputer will inform you with an error message of some sort. Here are some examples:

Mistake
Missing >
Missing "
Division by zero at line 10
No such line at line 30

Just as BASIC makes it easy to dissect strings, it is also easy to build them up. To illustrate this, you will need to store two character strings. Do this by first typing and entering:

S$ = "SKY"

Then type and enter:

T$ = "TRAIN"

Now see what you can build up from these strings. Try typing and

21

entering the following instruction:

PRINT S$ + T$

This instruction means 'print the string stored in S$ followed by the string stored in T$'. It gives:

SKYTRAIN

The following is a slightly more tricky instruction:

PRINT LEFT$(S$,2) + RIGHT$(T$,2)

Once it is typed and entered, it gives:

SKIN

In a similar fashion it is possible, using these two stored words, to get the BBC Microcomputer to print out a number of words, including 'INKY', 'TRAY', 'STAIN', 'STRAIN', 'STINKY'.

The BBC Microcomputer as a calculator

The BBC Microcomputer can be used like a calculator. If it seems to be a rather expensive calculator, remember that it is only one of the ways in which it can be used.

As you will realise by now, the number keys are situated on the top row of the keyboard. The arithmetic operation keys are labelled +, −, /, ★ and are to be found to the right-hand side of the keyboard. The symbol ★ is for multiplication to avoid confusion with the letter X, and / is for division because division sums must be typed out on one line. Arithmetic calculations can be performed by instructions such as the following:

PRINT 2+3+4

Once this is entered, it causes the answer to be printed as:

9

Another arithmetic instruction is:

PRINT (2★3+4)/5

Once this is entered, it gives:

2

Numbers can be stored using lines such as the following:

A = 3
B = 4

The result of this operation on the contents of memory is represented in Figure 2.5. Then you can give instructions merely using letters. For example:

PRINT A

gives:

3

Similarly:

PRINT A★B+8

gives:

20

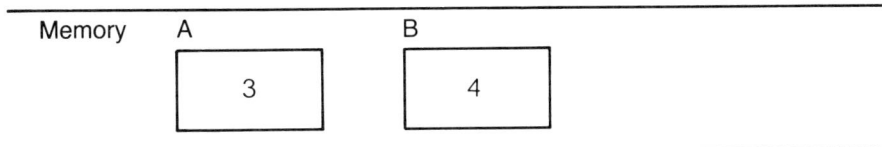

Figure 2.5 Numbers stored in the memory after A = 3: B = 4.

Summary

A good way to become familiar with the BBC Microcomputer's keyboard is to run a games program which requires responses to be made from the keyboard. A program can be loaded into the BBC Microcomputer's memory from a cassette by following the straightforward procedure initiated by giving the LOAD instruction. Once a program is loaded, it can be run. So, when starting to use the BBC Microcomputer, it is a good idea to practise with the programs available on the Welcome tape.

Most of the keys on the BBC Microcomputer's keyboard cause the corresponding symbol to appear on the screen when they are pressed, as one would expect. However, there are some keys which produce slight variations of the symbols, as compared with the symbol on the key itself. A little experimentation on the keyboard, soon gives an appreciation of the function of most of the keys.

Instructions can be given directly to the BBC Microcomputer in its own BASIC language. With the aid of a small repertoire of instructions, it is possible to instruct the BBC Microcomputer to perform such diverse activities as storing and manipulating words, and storing and manipulating numbers.

Self-test questions

1. What is the instruction which starts the procedure for loading a program into the BBC Microcomputer from a cassette?
2. Which keys provide the BBC Microcomputer's screen editing facilities? Using the fewest possible editing operations, how can the phrase:

   THE ASCENT OF MAN

be converted to:

   THE ANCIENT OMEN?

Also how can:

   BIRD LIVES

be converted to:

   BLIND MAN?

3. What instructions will cause the BBC Microcomputer to store the words 'LEAD' and 'POSE' using these stored words only? What instructions will cause the following words to be printed on the screen?

PLEAD,
POSED,
PLEASE,
LOSE,
ADDLE

4. Give instructions to cause the BBC Microcomputer to store the numbers 4 and 5. Give instructions involving these stored numbers only and operations on them, which produce the results 16, 24 and 36.

Chapter 3
Introduction to programming

Writing and running simple programs

A program is a sequence of instructions for a computer to obey. In order that the BBC Microcomputer may respond to such instructions, the language must be BASIC. You met a few examples of individual BASIC instructions in the previous chapter. BASIC is a simple programming language that was devised at Dartmouth College in the USA and first came into use in the early 1960s. It was intended to be easy to learn and to teach, and its overwhelming popularity as a language for microcomputers stems from the fact that it has been successful in this respect. You too will find it easy to learn.

The BBC Microcomputer first deals with a program by storing it. Then it can execute the program when instructed to do so, and as often and as many times as required. Or it can be modified, prior to being run again.

Since a program is a sequence of instructions, each instruction has to be numbered so as to tell the computer what the sequence is. Therefore each BASIC instruction within a program has to be preceded by a number. The computer then treats the number and the instruction together and stores them as a pair. It does not obey the instruction at the time of storing, but merely stores it for later action. So a computer program consists of a set of numbered instructions, and the numbers give the order in which the instructions are to be executed when the program is run. The instruction with the lowest number is the one to be executed first and so on. The numbers allow the instructions that make up the program to be entered in any order because the computer uses the numbers to put the instructions into the correct order.

This can be illustrated with the following short program to store the three words 'THE', 'DOG' and 'SHOW', and to use these stored words to print out the phrases 'THE DOG SHOW', 'SHOW THE DOG' and 'DOG THE SHOW':

```
10 A$ = "THE "
20 B$ = "DOG "
30 C$ = "SHOW "
```

```
40 CLS
50 PRINT A$+B$+C$
60 PRINT C$+A$+B$
70 PRINT B$+A$+C$
```

You will immediately notice that the line numbers start at 10 rather than 0 and go up in tens rather than one at a time. This is usual in computing because it allows you to insert at some later stage without having to renumber all the following lines to keep the order right. In this program the three words are stored in lines 10 to 30. Note that a space is included at the end of each word to act as a word-separator when the words are printed. Line 40 has the instruction CLS which causes the screen to be cleared of previous instructions or printing. Lines 50 to 70 cause the required phrases to be printed. Figure 3.1 shows the consequence of executing each instruction of the program. The result of running the program is the cumulative effect produced by executing each of its instructions.

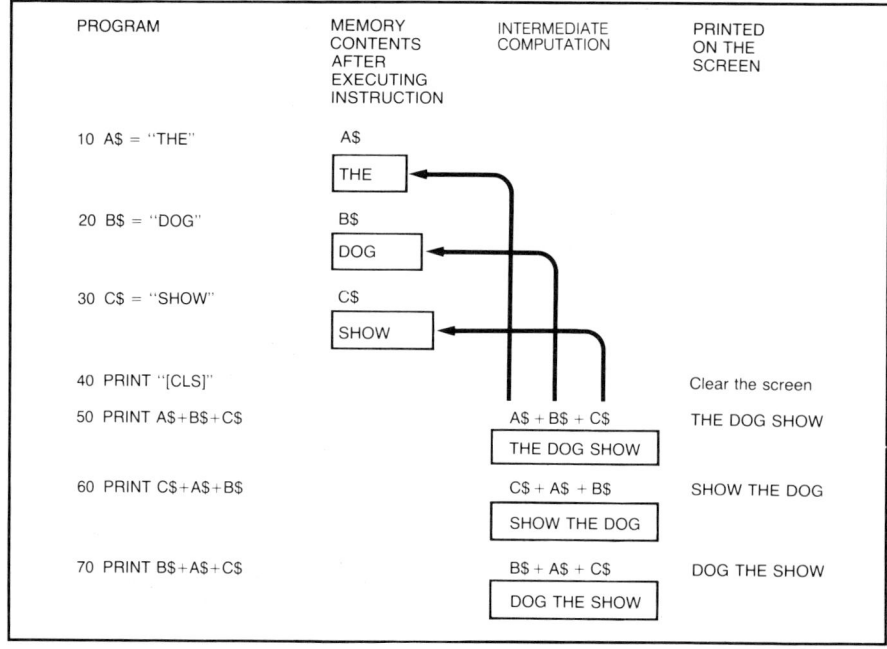

Figure 3.1 The results of running a program.

Before putting this program into the computer, it is a good idea to type and enter NEW (i.e. type NEW, then press the RETURN key) because this clears any program lines previously stored in the computer. Then type the program exactly as shown, pressing the RETURN key at the end of each line to enter it, i.e. to cause it to be stored in the computer.

To demonstrate that the program has been stored by the computer, type and enter:

LIST

In response to this, the BBC Microcomputer always lists the program it is storing. Check the listing given on the screen against the listing in this book to see if they agree exactly. If they do, execute the program by typing and entering:

RUN

You will then see the results of the program looking like this:

```
THE DOG SHOW
SHOW THE DOG
DOG THE SHOW
>-
```

Remember that because the program is stored in the BBC Microcomputer, it can be listed or executed as often as you like. If a line of the program has been entered incorrectly, you can correct it by first listing and then using the editing facilities as explained in the last chapter. Suppose that line 20 happened to need editing because it has been mistakenly entered as:

20 B$="DIG"

You can correct it by using the CURSOR CONTROL keys to position the flashing cursor at the beginning of the line, on the number 2. Then press the COPY key until the flashing cursor arrives under the letter G. At this stage the newly edited version, copied at the bottom of the screen, would be:

```
20 B$="DI
```

Now press the DELETE key. This removes the I from the screen. Type O from the keyboard, followed by two presses of the 'copy' key to copy in the rest of the line to produce the final corrected version. Pressing RETURN causes this corrected line to be stored by the computer just as if it had been entered like that from the keyboard first time round. You can confirm this by listing the program. Then you will see the corrected program in the normal way. Note that some programs may be so long that the erroneous line is listed off the screen. Thus, before you can edit it, you have to bring it on to the screen by typing and entering

LIST 20

Another way of editing a program is to retype a line completely. Merely type and enter the new version. For example, typing and entering the following new line 30 causes this new line to replace the previous line 30, as you can confirm by listing:

30 C$="HOUSE"

To delete a line, all that is necessary is to type and enter the number of the line to be removed. For example, try typing and entering just:

60

Then, to see the effect, type and enter:

LIST

When you have finished experimenting with the program, type and enter the following, to delete the complete program and prepare the computer for a new program:

NEW

Check that the LIST instruction now evokes no response. If you happen to enter NEW by mistake, you can recover your previous program by typing and entering:

OLD

This method of recovery of an old program only works so long as you have not entered any new program lines.

Giving data to a program while it is running

This section and the next two sections introduce a few more BASIC instructions. They are incorporated into short programs to illustrate their usefulness. When putting the programs into the computer, the RETURN key has to be pressed after each line to enter it; otherwise the BBC Microcomputer will take no action. Remember this point as you read on, because it will no longer always be explicitly mentioned! So if you have typed something out, and nothing seems to be happening as you sit and wait, ask yourself whether you have pressed the RETURN key!

Suppose that you would like to modify the program about 'THE', 'DOG' and 'SHOW' so that it accepts any three words typed on the keyboard while the program is running. That is, you want the computer to accept an input from the keyboard while the program is running. The instruction is:

INPUT

When an INPUT instruction is executed, it causes a question mark to be printed on the screen to indicate that the user should give a response in the form of typing on the keyboard. Then the BBC Microcomputer will wait until the user types this response, which it will then accept. Thus the following instruction produces a question mark to be printed on the screen:

10 INPUT A$

Suppose that the user types and enters:

THE

The computer accepts the word 'THE' and stores it in A$. The effect is the same as that of the following instruction:

10 A$ = "THE"

However, whereas the latter always gives A$ the value 'THE', the former can be whatever the user types.

The new program can be based on the previous one by replacing the lines that store the three words with three INPUT instructions, one for each word. When the three words have been entered in this way, lines 50 to 70 will print them out as phrases, as they did before. Note that when a word is entered using an INPUT instruction, the computer ignores any spaces before the first letter. Almost certainly the user will type in the words without spaces in front of them; so the program must itself provide the spaces. This is done in the following program which will accept any three words and will then print three phrases involving them.

```
10 CLS
20 INPUT A$
30 INPUT B$
40 INPUT C$
50 PRINT A$+" "+B$+" "+C$
```

```
60 PRINT C$+" "+A$+" "+B$
70 PRINT B$+" "+A$+" "+C$
```

When this program is executed it might result in a dialogue like the following:

```
?THE
?KIT
?BAG
THE KIT BAG
BAG THE KIT
KIT THE BAG
```

Making decisions in programs

The BBC Microcomputer can be programmed to make decisions — and this can be used to produce some very interesting programs. The instruction which permits decision-making uses the BASIC words IF and THEN. It has the form:

    IF condition THEN action

In the 'condition' part, variables and/or values can be compared. This could typically be to see if two values were the same or not. The 'action' part can be any valid BASIC instruction. An example of such an 'action' could be perhaps a print instruction.

When executed, the computer tests the condition part and, if the condition holds, then it executes the action part. If the condition part does not hold, then the instruction part will not be executed. An example of this type of instruction is:

IF N$ = "PASSWORD" THEN PRINT "ACCEPTED"

When this is executed, the BBC Microcomputer tests to see whether the most recent value of N$ is PASSWORD. If it is, then the following appears on the screen:

ACCEPTED

If it is not accepted, then nothing happens.

    A second example is as follows, where the pair of symbols <> mean 'not equal to':

IF N$ <> "PASSWORD" THEN PRINT "REJECTED"

Thus when this instruction is executed, REJECTED is printed only if the most recent value of N$ is not PASSWORD.

Any one test can have two possible outcomes. BASIC allows for this in an instruction of the following form:

IF condition THEN action 1 ELSE action 2

The following is this combined form for the two previous examples:

IF N$ = "PASSWORD" THEN PRINT "ACCEPTED" ELSE PRINT "REJECTED"

Now consider a short program to create a sum, display it, accept an answer to it and decide whether or not the answer is correct. This should then be followed by the printing of an appropriate message. The plan for this program is shown in Figure 3.2 which is an example of what is called a

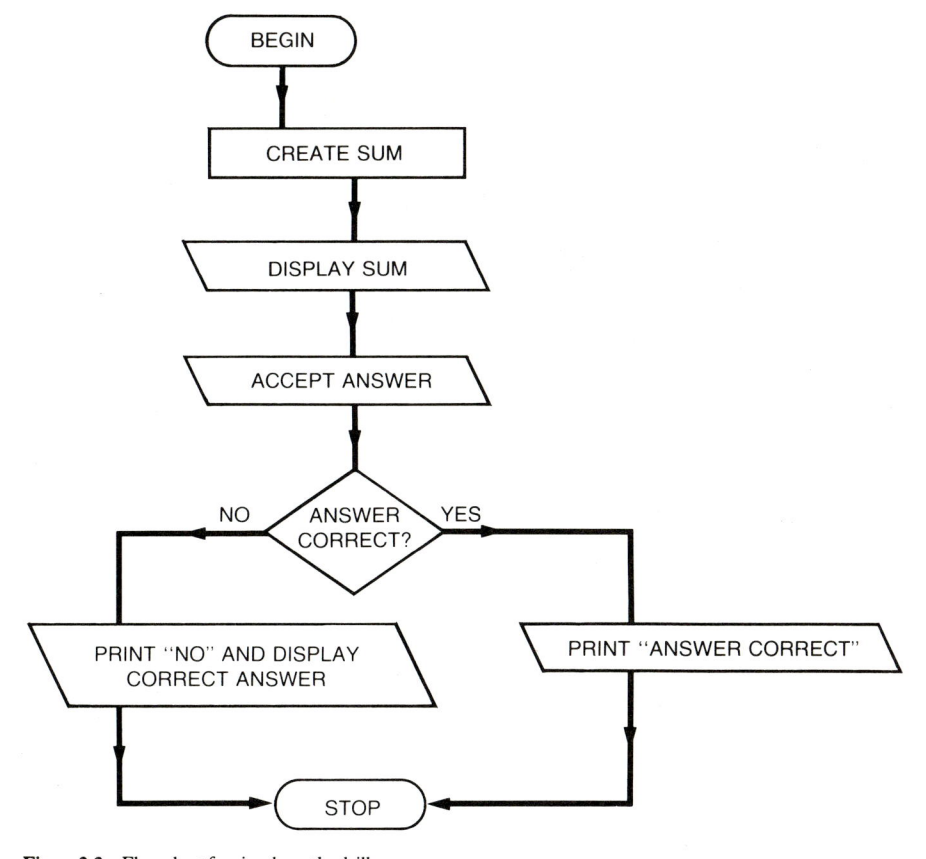

Figure 3.2 Flow chart for simple maths drill program.

flowchart.

The program starts by storing two numbers in A and B. Then line 30 uses these numbers to print out a question about their sum. This question is:

WHAT IS 2+3?

Since the various items are to appear on the screen with no spaces between them, a semi-colon is used to separate them in the PRINT instruction. (With a comma separating them in the PRINT instruction, they would be printed on the screen separated by spaces.) Line 40 accepts a number from the keyboard and stores it in C. Then, in line 50, the offered answer is tested to see if it is equal to the actual answer. If it is, then an encouraging message is printed. The final line detects when the wrong answer is given, and causes the real answer to be printed. The program is:

```
10  A=2
20  B=3
30  PRINT "What is ";A;" + ";B;" ?"
40  INPUT C
50  IF C = A+B THEN PRINT "good. That is correct"
60  IF C <> A+B THEN PRINT "No. The answer is ";A+B
```

By using a GOTO instruction, the program can be adapted to give the user more than one attempt to find the answer. This is illustrated in Figure 3.3. A GOTO instruction tells the computer to skip lines of program and go immediately to a certain program line. For example, the following tells the computer to go to line 30 and execute that line next:

GOTO 30

The previous program can be modified by the use of GOTO to produce a program which expects the user to keep trying until he finds the correct answer. Line 50 has to be replaced by one which tests for the correct answer. This uses a GOTO instruction to branch to the last line of the program which prints up a congratulatory message. Line 60, which is only reached if the incorrect answer gets offered, prints up a message saying that the answer is wrong and inviting the user to try again. The next line again uses a GOTO instruction to take the program operation back to line 30, ready for the whole process to be repeated again.

```
10  A=2
20  B=3
30  PRINT "What is ";A;"+ ;B;"?"
40  INPUT C
```

```
50  IF C=A+B THEN GOTO 80
60  PRINT "Sorry, wrong answer. Try again"
70  GOTO 30
80  PRINT "Good. That is correct"
```

The following is typical of a dialogue produced by this program:

What is 2+3?
? 6
Sorry, wrong answer. Try again
What is 2+3?
? 4
Sorry, wrong answer. Try again
What is 2+3?
? 5
Good. That is correct.

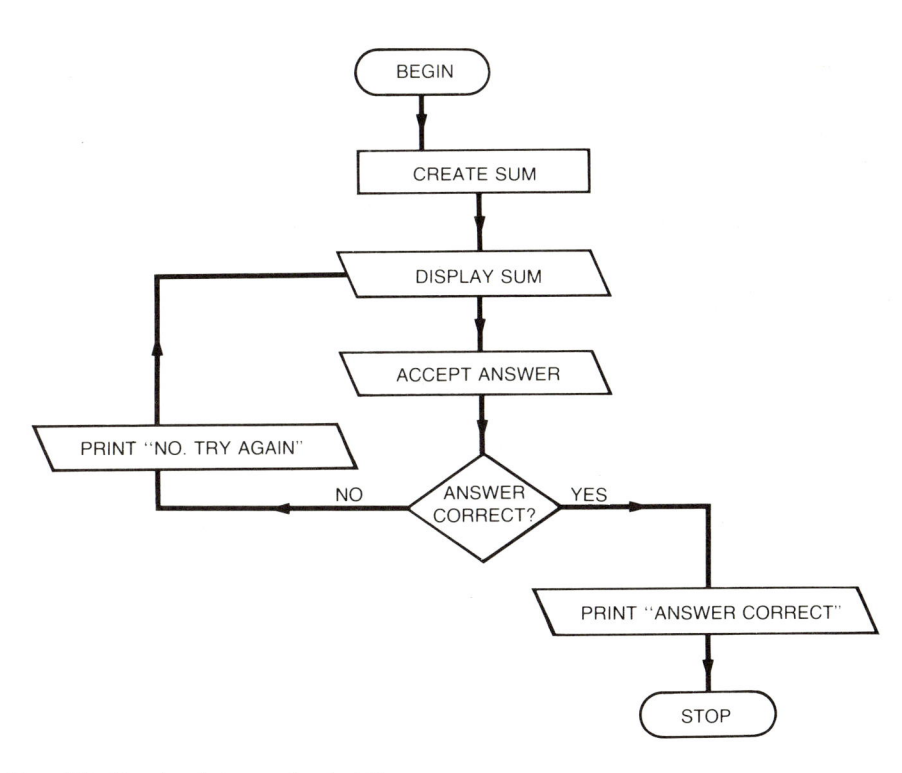

Figure 3.3 Flow chart for improved maths drill program.

Repetition in programs

As you saw from the previous program, the BBC Microcomputer can be programmed to do things repeatedly by using the GOTO instruction. Thus the problem gets posed repeatedly until the correct answer is given. However, BASIC has a more direct way to achieve repetition. This is using the words FOR and NEXT. Their use is illustrated in the following program:

```
10 FOR I = 1 TO 16
20 PRINT "JILL"
30 NEXT I
```

This program causes JILL to be printed sixteen times because all the instructions between the FOR and NEXT are repeated as many times as directed by the FOR instruction. In this case the FOR instruction directs the BBC Microcomputer to do the first repetition with I=1; the next with I=2; and so on until the last repetition with I=16.

The next program illustrates that you can put as many instructions as required between the FOR and NEXT:

```
10 FOR K = 1 TO 9
20 PRINT "Repetition number =";K
30 PRINT "Frances"
40 PRINT
50 NEXT K
```

This causes nine repetitions and produces the following to appear on the screen:

```
Repetition number 1
Frances

Repetition number 2
Frances

. . .
```

This continues up to the ninth repetition.

You can now write a program to accept a word and to spell out all of its letters, one at a time. The program must ask for a word, accept it, find its length and then repeatedly pick out and print the first letter, second letter and so on until the last letter. You already know how to separate letters from the left or the right of a word. BASIC also provides a way to examine the middle of a word with MID$. It works like this. The following instruction gives A$ part of the word assigned to N$.

A$=MID$(N$,2,4)

The extracted part starts with the second letter and is four letters long. By way of illustration, the following lines give ANNE:

10 J$="JOANNE"
20 PRINT MID$(J$,3,4)

While the following lines give RAN:

30 F$="FRANCES"
40 PRINT MID$(F$,2,3)

This gives all the equipment to write the program. The program will start with a polite request to enter a word, and this will be followed by an INPUT instruction to accept and store the word in W$. At line 30 the number of letters in the word is found, and stored in L. Note that line 50 contains MID$(W$,I,1). Now MID$(W$,3,1) will extract a string of letters from the word stored in W$. It starts with the third letter from the beginning and is one letter long, which means that it finds the third letter of the stored word. Therefore the effect of lines 40 to 60 is to find repeatedly the successive letters of the word and print out that letter. Number one is whatever the first letter is and so on. The following is the entire program for spelling out all the letters which make up a word:

10 PRINT "Enter a word, please"
20 INPUT W$
30 L=LEN(W$)
40 FOR I=1 TO L
50 PRINT "Letter number ";I;" is ";MID$(W$,I,1)
60 NEXT I

More programs

Suppose you want to write a program to accept any name in the form of a first name followed by a surname, for example:

JAMES JOYCE

Suppose that you want a printout of the form:

your first name is JAMES
your surname is JOYCE

At first sight, this may seem very easy. You may think that, after using the instruction INPUT N$ to get in the name, the first name can be given by LEFT$(N$,5) and the surname by RIGHT$(N$,5). Unfortunately this will produce nonsense if the names are not five letters long, for example if they are something like PATRICK CAMPBELL.

What is actually needed is to locate the position of the space which separates the two parts of the name. Then, assuming that the name has been entered correctly, everything to the left of the space must be the first name and everything to the right must be the surname. Even then, if the name is not entered in the expected way, strange results can still be printed. So it is sensible to request that the name be entered in standard fashion and then to check the entered name, rejecting it if it does not conform. This reasoning leads to the following program:

```
10  CLS
20  PRINT "Enter your name, please. Type"
30  PRINT "your first name, then one"
40  PRINT "space then your second name."
50  INPUT N$
60  L = LEN (N$) : C = 0
70  FOR I = 1 TO L
80  IF MID$(N$,I,1) = " " THEN C=C+1
90  NEXT I
100 IF C <> 1 THEN PRINT "Please enter your name as requested."
110 IF C<> 1 THEN GOTO 20
120 FOR J = 1 TO L
130 IF MID$(N$,J,1) = " " THEN B=J
140 NEXT J
150 PRINT "Your first name is ";LEFT$(N$,B−1)
160 PRINT "Your surname is ";RIGHT$(N$,L−B)
```

This program starts by clearing the screen. Lines 20 to 40 cause the instructions for using the program to be printed on the screen and line 50 accepts a name and stores it in N$. Line 60 contains two instructions, which are separated by a colon. The first instruction stores the number of characters in the name in L. The second sets the starting value of C to zero. This is then used to count the number of spaces in the name. Lines 70 to 90 scan each character in the name, counting the number of spaces. At the end of the repetitions, the number of spaces in the name is held in C. If there is no single space in the name, then lines 100 to 110 indicate that the entry is not satisfactory and cause the program to go back to line 20 to ask for the name to entered again. Lines 120 to 140 locate the position of the space, storing it in B so that line 150 can print all the characters to the left of the space as the first name, and line 160 can print all those to the right as the surname.

The next program produces a rather fascinating mobile display of a worm-like object which moves backwards and forwards across the screen. The shape of the worm is stored in the string A$, in the first line. This shape is preceded by thirty spaces and followed by one space. Lines 30 to 50 cause it to move from left to right by repetitively printing increasingly longer strings taken from the right of the string. In other words the worm is printed with more and more spaces. Lines 60 to 80 move it in the other direction.

When, in a FOR instruction such as the one in line 30, no step is mentioned, I increases from four to the value of L in steps of one. However at line 60 a step is mentioned, so that the value of J for the first repetition is the value of L. This value is changed by -1 until the value four is reached on the last repetition. If the space at the end of the string in line 10 is removed, the shape will leave a trail when it moves from right to left. This is eaten up again during movement in the opposite direction. The complete mobile display program is:

```
10  A$ = "                      XXX "
20  L = LEN(A$) : B$ = CH$(13)
30  FOR I = 4 TO L
40  PRINT B$;RIGHT$(A$,I);
50  NEXT I
60  FOR J = L TO 4 STEP −1
70  PRINT B$;RIGHT$(A$,J);
80  NEXTJ
90  GOTO 30
```

The last line of this program always causes the program to start again at line 00 which is the start of the worm drawing routine. So it starts the worm on another pass across the screen. The program runs indefinitely when executed. To stop it, you have to press the ESCAPE key.

You can now develop a program to translate French words to their English equivalents. To do this you need to store French words and the corresponding English words, in such a way that the English and French equivalent words can be related to each other. This is a suitable opportunity for introducing the idea of an 'array' which is useful for manipulating lists. It requires a BASIC instruction like:

DIM A$(20)

This means that you want to establish twenty variables to which words can be assigned. Their names are A$(1), A$(2), . . . A$(20) etc., and they can be used in the same way as ordinary variables. The following is such an assignment:

A$(6) = "MAN"

The DIM instruction also reserves storage space for all the variables in the array. As the following program shows, arrays can be used to advantage in FOR . . . NEXT repetitions. The following program uses two arrays, as illustrated in Figure 3.4, one holding French words and the other holding the equivalent English words in the same order. The program translates by seeking to match the French word to be translated with one of the French words stored in the array F$. If a match is found, then the word is translated to the English word in the corresponding position in the array E$. In the program, line 10 reserves space for the two arrays, which will hold the French and English words. The words themselves are stored by lines 20 to 50, and when the lines up to 50 have been executed, the state of the memory is as represented in Figure 3.4.

Line 60 requests the entry of a French word and line 70 accepts it and stores it. Line 80 sets the variable T to zero. It will stay zero unless a match is found for the entered French word, so that it can be translated. Lines 90 to 120 search the entire stored French vocabulary for a match to the entered word. If a match is found, then the corresponding English word is printed by line 100 while T is changed to 1 by line 110. After these repetitions, line 130 tests T. If T is still zero, the word cannot be translated and an appropriate message is produced. Line 140 causes line 60 to be executed next, so that another French word can be entered and the subsequent part of the program can be repeated. The program for translating French words to English is as follows:

```
10 DIM E$(4), F$(4)
20 E$(1)="MAN":F$(1)="HOMME"
30 E$(2)="WOMAN":F$(2)="FEMME"
40 E$(3)="BOY":F$(3)="GARCON"
50 E$(4)="GIRL":F$(4)="JEUNE FILLE"
```

	E$(1)	E$(2)	E$(3)	E$(4)
E$	MAN	WOMAN	BOY	GIRL

	F$(1)	F$(2)	F$(3)	F$(4)
F$	HOMME	FEMME	GARCON	JEUNE FILLE

Figure 3.4 Two parallel arrays for translation program.

```
 60 PRINT "Enter french word"
 70 INPUT W$
 80 T=0
 90 FOR I = 1 TO 4
100 IF W$=F$(I)THEN PRINT E$(I)
110 IF W$=F$(I)THEN T=1
120 NEXT I
130 IF T=0 THEN PRINT W$;" is not in my vocabulary"
140 GOTO 60
```

Clearly, as presented here, this program has a very limited vocabulary. However, this can be extended in a straightforward way. Also, the program is not difficult to adapt so that it translates from English to French. You can experiment with it and see what you can make it do. In fact all the programs presented in this section can be used as vehicles for experimenting with programming in BASIC. They can be amended, extended and improved in many ways.

Saving programs

When the BBC Microcomputer is switched off, the program stored in it is lost. To avoid having to type a program in every time that you want to use it and to preserve a record of it, you have to copy it into some form of permanent storage. This process is called 'saving'. With the BBC Microcomputer a program can be saved using either a cassette unit or a disk unit. Then it can be loaded again at another time.

To save a program on cassette, first attach the cassette unit to the computer, and put a blank cassette into it. Completely rewind the tape and then wind it forwards a little to avoid trying to record on the tape leader. Decide on a name for your program, for example, TRANSLATOR, and then, when the tape is positioned properly, type and enter:

SAVE "TRANSLATOR"

This produces the message:

RECORD then RETURN

When you press the RETURN key, nothing appears to happen for a few seconds because, during this time, the BBC Microcomputer is writing a continuous tone on the cassette tape to separate one program from the next on the tape. When the program itself starts to be recorded on the tape, the name of the program will be printed up on the screen as follows:

As the program gets written to the cassette tape, the numbers after the name change. When the recording on the tape is complete, the normal cursor reappears on the screen. It is possible, and advisable, to verify that the program has been copied correctly on to the tape, as one small error can ruin a whole program. To do this, rewind the cassette and type:

★CAT

Then set the tape recorder to play. Each time the BBC Microcomputer comes across a new program recorded on the tape, it will print the name of that program and report any errors that it comes across as error messages. If no error messages occur, then you can take it that the program has been recorded correctly. Now press the ESCAPE key to get back to the normal mode of working. This is necessary, because when the computer is given the instruction ★CAT, it will actually search through the whole of the cassette tape looking to see what programs are on it, while at the same time, verifying that they are all in the correct format. If it finds any errors, it will give an error message. If the verification fails, you have to restart the

```
>SAVE  "TRANSLATOR"
RECORD then RETURN
TRANSLATOR 07 07DB
>_
```

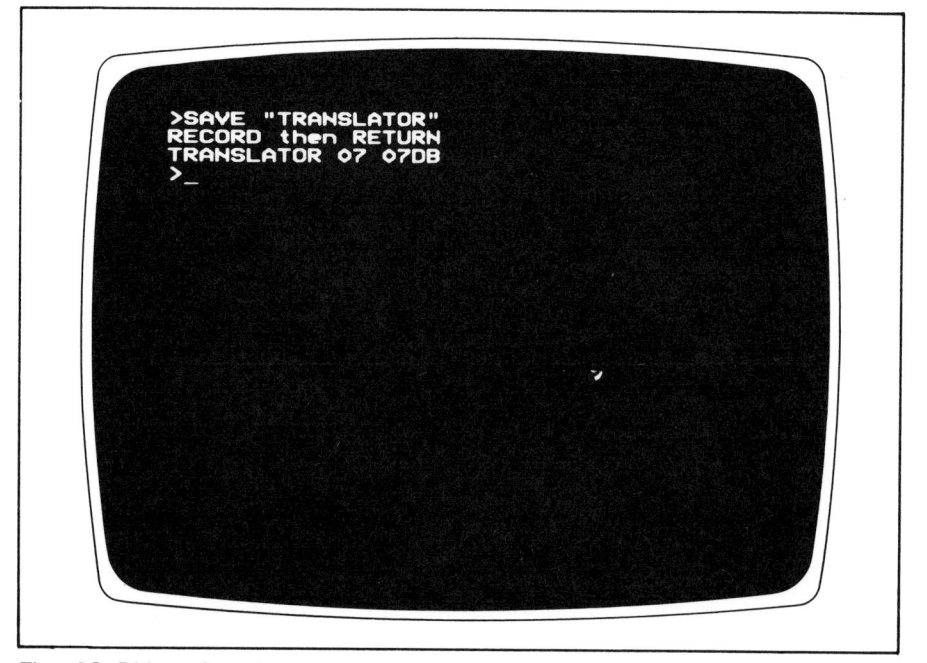

Figure 3.5   Dialogue after saving a program.

entire procedure for saving the program. The screen dialogue, after successfully saving a program, is shown in Figure 3.5.

Using the printer

Using a printer with the BBC Microcomputer can considerably enhance its performance. Initially the main uses for a printer are probably to provide listings of programs and to print results in a permanent and convenient form. Program listings on paper are not only a convenient record but can also be taken away from the computer and studied at leisure. If a program produces a lot of results, it is more convenient to print them out than to copy them from the screen, and it is also more reliable.

After the initial precautions of insuring that the printer is attached to the BBC Microcomputer, is switched on and loaded with paper, you can list the stored program on the printer as well as on the screen. The instruction to turn the printer on is:

PRINT CHR$(2)

It is turned off again by:

PRINT CHR$(3)

While the printer is turned on, all the output which is normally printed to the screen is printed both to the screen and to the printer. Thus everything you type on the keyboard will be sent to the printer as well as to the screen.

Summary

The BBC Microcomputer can store a BASIC program which can either be executed as often as required or which can be modified before it is run again. The BBC Microcomputer's BASIC language is a simple English-like language which provides, among other things, facilities for storing and manipulating information, for making decisions and for repeating actions as often as required. This chapter introduced these BASIC instructions and illustrated their use by incorporating them into programs.

When a program has been written, it can be saved on cassette tape or disk. This chapter has described how this can be done for cassette tape. It has also described the use of a printer.

Self-test questions

1. What is the instruction to start the procedure for saving a program stored in the BBC Microcomputer onto cassette tape?

2. What are the BASIC terms for:
   a) repetition?
   b) making a test and acting on the results?
   c) giving data to a program while it is running?

3. Write short programs to do the following:
   a) to print your name ten times;
   b) to enter a word and decide if it has more than seven characters. If it has more than seven characters, indicate that a long word was entered. Otherwise print that it was a short one;
   c) to repetitively accept a word and then print it out without either its first or last letter.

4. Explain in the way illustrated in Figure 3.1, the computations performed when the following programs are executed:

a) 10 A$ = "ALGORITHMIC"
   20 L = LEN(A$)
   30 FOR I = 1 TO L
   40 PRINT LEFT$(A$,I)
   50 NEXT I

b) 10 A = 1: B = 1
   20 PRINT A: PRINT B
   30 FOR I = 1 TO 12
   40 C = A+B
   50 PRINT C
   60 A = B: B = C
   70 NEXT I

5. Write a program to accept a word, store it in A$, and then create in B$ the reverse of the word. This can be done by starting with a string of zero characters in B$, and then adding one character at a time from the right of

A$. The program should print the reversed word, and then decide if the original word reads the same forwards and backwards. (Words that do this are called palindromes.)

A typical dialogue from the program might be:

ENTER A WORD, PLEASE
?MADAM
THE REVERSE OF MADAM IS MADAM
MADAM IS PALINDROMIC.

Chapter 4
Coloured writing and graphics

Coloured writing

The BBC Microcomputer is renowned for the coloured display that it can produce. To make full use of it, you need a colour television, but if you only have a black and white one, you can still get sufficiently different shades of grey for attractive effects.

Before you can use any colours, you need to choose to work in one of what are called 'modes'. Several are available. They allow you to have either 20, 40 or 80 characters per line, with either 25 or 32 lines per screen. The mode in which the BBC Microcomputer finds itself when first turned on is called mode 7. It allows 25 lines, each of 40 characters and it displays text with the same character set as the television Teletext: Oracle and Ceefax. In just a few instances, you will find that these characters are slightly different from those labelled on the keyboard, but the instances will be too few to cause any major problems.

It is probably best for you to start learning about colour by working in mode 5. This provides 32 lines of 20 text characters. When you turn on, you can get into mode 5 with the following instruction:

MODE 5

When this is entered, the screen will clear and any typed characters will appear larger than they were in mode 7. This is because there are now only 20 characters per line.

In mode 5, you can choose to write characters in any of the following four colours:

    black
    red
    yellow
    white

You can choose the foreground and background colour independently.

Choose one of the following instructions for defining the foreground colour, according to whether you want it to be black, red, yellow or white:

COLOUR 0 (which defines the foreground colour as black)

COLOUR 1 (which defines the foreground colour as red)
COLOUR 2 (which defines the foreground colour as yellow)
COLOUR 3 (which defines the foreground colour as white)

In other modes, with a different number of colours available, there are a corresponding number of COLOUR instructions. (Details of the facilities available in the various modes can be found in Chapter 5 under the heading Specification of the BBC Microcomputer.)

For the background colour, you need one of the following COLOUR instructions:

COLOUR 128 (which defines the background colour as black)
COLOUR 129 (which defines the background colour as red)
COLOUR 130 (which defines the background colour as yellow)
COLOUR 131 (which defines the background colour as white)

As an example of how to set the colour of the display, consider a program which prints up a simple message in yellow writing on a red background. As listed above, the instruction COLOUR 2 sets the writing (i.e. the foreground) to yellow and COLOUR 129 sets the background to red. Suppose you want to print the following message in yellow on a red background:

WELCOME

This is achieved by the following few lines:

10 MODE 5
20 COLOUR 2
30 COLOUR 129
40 PRINT "WELCOME"

You will find that the screen starts off black. Only where the writing appears will the red background and yellow foreground be set. If you would like to clear the screen of all previous writing and also set its overall colour, then start with the instruction CLS to clear the screen.

Suppose you want black writing on a white background. The foreground colour has to be set by COLOUR 0, and the background has to be set by COLOUR 131. The previous message can be written in black with the following program:

10 MODE 5
20 COLOUR 0
30 COLOUR 131
40 CLS
50 PRINT "WELCOME"

Note that line 20 sets the foreground to black, while the overall screen colour has been set to white by lines 30 and 40.

Next comes a program which demonstrates writing on the screen in all possible combinations of foreground and background colours. It generates a rather pretty and unusual pattern, because characters seem to disappear when the foreground and background colours are the same. Before you look at a listing of the program, you need to know about one new feature which it uses. This is the *random number generator*. Nearly all computers have some means of generating random numbers. With the BBC Microcomputer a random number between 1 and 4 is generated by the following instruction:

RND(4)

The pattern-generating program uses this to produce a foreground with a colour number that keeps randomly changing. The complete program is:

```
10  MODE 5
20  FOR X=0 TO 620
30  COLOUR RND(4)−1
40  COLOUR RND(4)+127
50  PRINT "X";
60  NEXT X
70  COLOUR 3
80  COLOUR 128
```

Line 10 sets the display mode, while lines 30 and 40 generate random foreground and background colours. Lines 70 and 80 are important as they return the display to normal when the program is finished. If you do not arrange for this, it is quite possible for the computer to appear not to respond to the keyboard. This can happen when the writing is invisible due to identical foreground and background colours.

Coloured pictures

In computer terminology, pictures of any kind are known as 'graphics'. Most of the programs written for the BBC Microcomputer and of lasting interest and value will make use of graphics. It can be argued that much of the interest and compulsion of games and educational programs lies in their imaginative use of pictures. Business programs can be much more effective if they present information and results in pictorial as well as numerical form. This is not to say that some numerical computation will not be necessary in any reasonably complex program.

The results from a program can be presented in one of three ways: with numbers, in words or by pictures. While in some applications, it is essential to have the detailed numerical results printed out, this inevitably looks rather dull. To present information using words is perhaps better, but books are easier to read than are video screens. Anyway, as everybody knows, a picture is worth a thousand words and pictorial presentations are much more natural and informative than their alternatives.

The screen and memory

To make it easy to use the graphics, the BBC Microcomputer has two methods of drawing on the screen. In the method considered now, which is the one used when the computer is first turned on, the screen is what is called 'memory mapped'. The idea is that each position in which a letter, number or graphics character can be placed should correspond to a location in a particular part of the computer's memory. By placing a number in a location in this area of memory, the appropriate character appears on the corresponding screen position. This produces a graphics display which is actually a memory management exercise.

When the computer is first turned on, the display occupies just 1000 memory locations. The 1000 character positions on the screen correspond to the 1000 memory locations numbered from 31744 to 32743. The position of the top left-hand corner of the screen corresponds to location 31744 and the bottom right-hand corner corresponds to location 32743. The correspondence of the other screen positions and memory locations is shown in Figure 4.1. In fact at all times the BBC Microcomputer generates its screen display by examining an area of memory and producing the display corresponding to what is stored in it.

It is useful to be able to work out the number of the memory location corresponding to any screen position. You can do this with the aid of Figure 4.1. Observe that on the top row, the first character position corresponds to location 31744; the second to 31744+1; the third to 31744+2, and so on. Consequently, in this row, the character positions in any column correspond to location 31744 plus 1 less than the column number. Similarly, in the first row, the screen position corresponds to 31744; the second to 31744 + 40; the third to 31744 + 2 ★ 40; and so on. (This is because there are forty character positions in a row.) Thus, in this column, the character position in any row corresponds to location 31744 + 40 ★ (1 less than the row number). Therefore the number of the memory

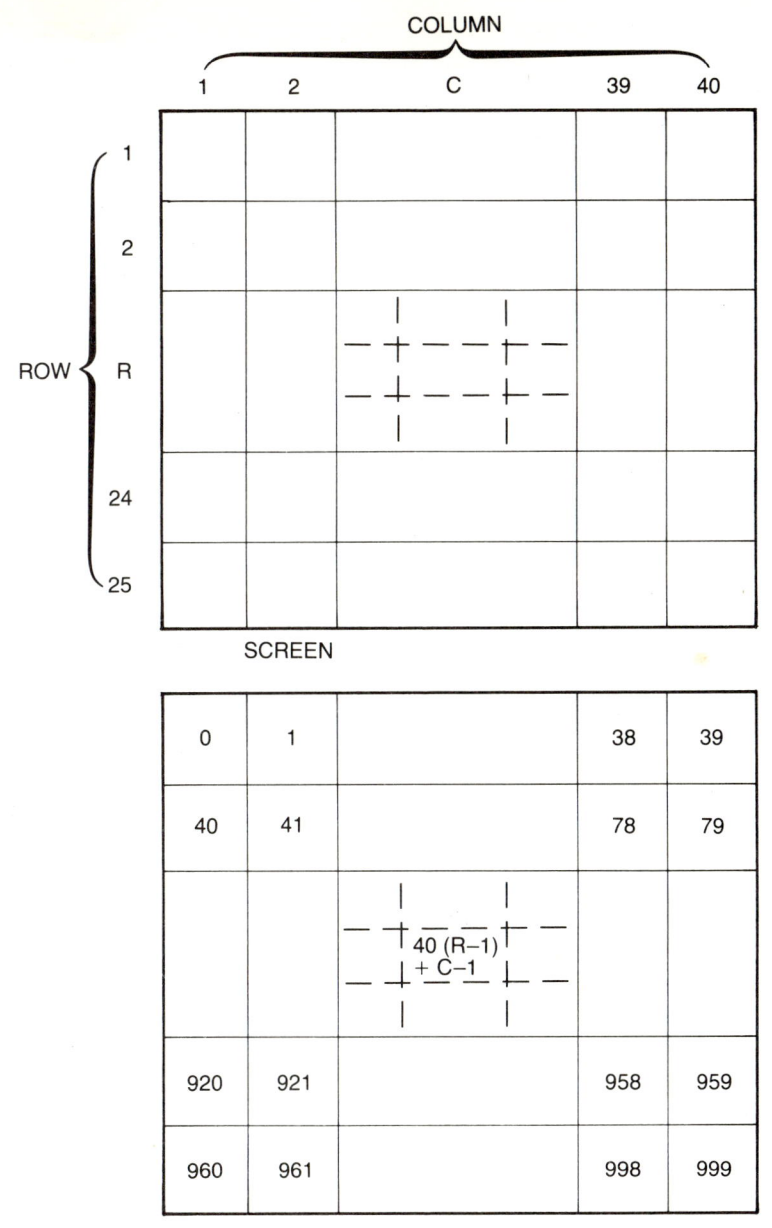

MEMORY LOCATIONS ARRANGED AS MAPPED TO THE SCREEN.
ADD 31744 TO THE NUMBER WRITTEN IN EACH LOCATION TO OBTAIN
THE ADDRESS OF THAT LOCATION

Figure 4.1 Memory map for the BBC Microcomputer screen.

location corresponding to a screen element in a particular row and column equals 31744 + 40 ★ (row number minus 1) + (column number minus 1).

Putting a character on the screen

With the BBC Microcomputer, you can put characters on to the screen by several methods. One way is by using an instruction which allows information to be put directly into the memory of the computer's memory-mapped display. As an example the following instruction causes the number 42 to be stored in location 31744:

Figure 4.2 Table of the teletext graphics characters and their codes.

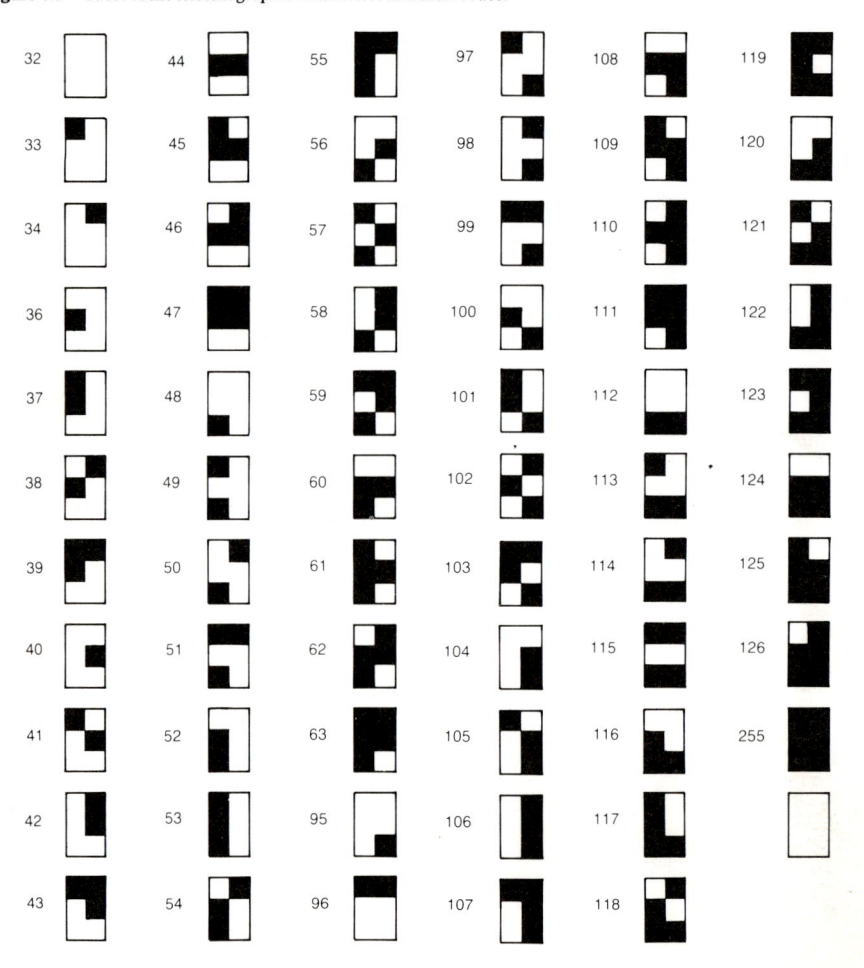

?31744 = 42

Location 31744 corresponds to the position at the top left-hand corner of the screen, and 42 is the code for an asterisk. So an asterisk appears at the top left of the screen. Thus the principal effect of this instruction is to store a number in a memory location. If that location corresponds to a screen position, then the secondary effect is to cause the character whose code is that number to appear in the corresponding position on the screen.

As already mentioned, when the BBC Microcomputer is first turned on, it is in mode 7 which is compatible with the Teletext characters of Ceefax and Oracle. Accordingly it will display a graphics character on any line which starts with the code 147. Figure 4.2 gives a table of such graphics characters together with their code numbers.

Producing a drawing

This section describes a way of sketching a simple recognisable shape on the screen. It also demonstrates that mode 7 has only a medium

Figure 4.3 (a) Butterfly. (b) Butterfly with grid. (c) Butterfly composed of graphics characters. (d) Outline of image plotted on screen.

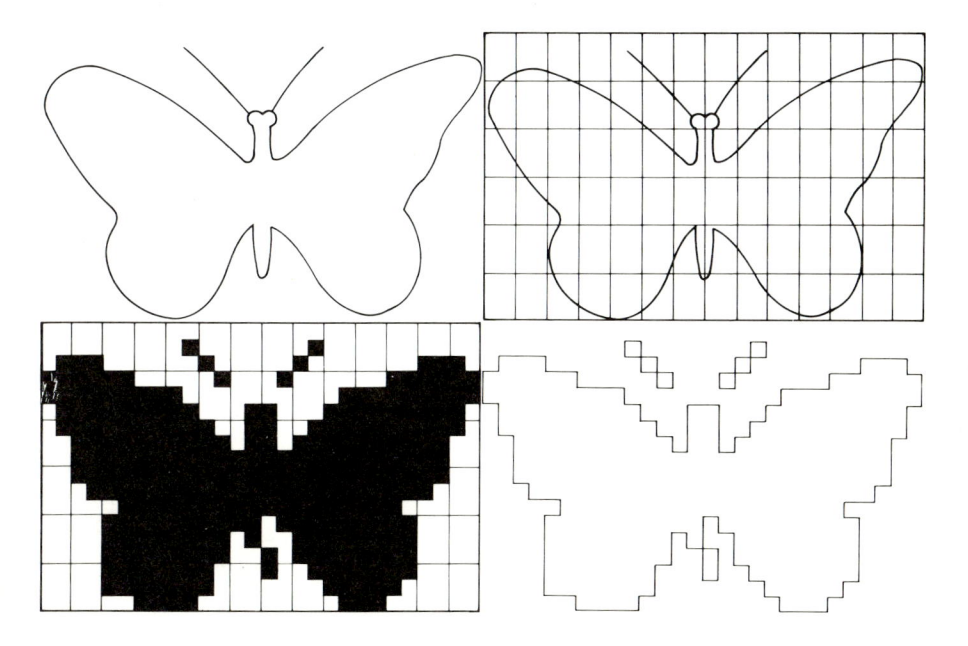

51

'resolution' which means that it can show only moderate detail.

Suppose you want to draw the butterfly illustrated in Figure 4.3a. First draw a square grid over it, as shown in Figure 4.3b and then find the graphics character which most closely resembles the shape in each square in the grid. This is shown in Figure 4.3c. The outline of the butterfly as it would be drawn on the BBC Microcomputer's screen is shown in Figure 4.3d. Finally find the codes for the graphics symbols.

Writing a program to put these codes into the appropriate locations requires the BASIC terms READ and DATA. The names are fairly self-explanatory. A READ instruction reads information from lines called DATA instructions. The first READ instruction executed in a program reads the first DATA item; the second READ instruction takes the second item; and so on. Using these features, you can write the codes of the characters which make up the butterfly in DATA lists, and read them as required. The following is a suitable program. It draws the butterfly in a 6 by 14 block of screen positions near the centre of the screen.

```
 10 CLS
 20 S=31744+8*40+13
 30 FOR R=1 TO 6
 40 FOR C=1 TO 15
 50 READ A
 60 ?(S+C)=A
 70 NEXT C
 80 S=S+40
 90 NEXT R
100 DATA
    147,120,124,112,32,32,41,48,224,38,32,224,112,124,116
110 DATA
    147,107,255,255,255,125,48,104,52,224,126,255,255,255,55
120 DATA
    147,32,255,255,255,255,255,126,125,255,255,255,255,53,32
130 DATA
    147,32,34,123,255,255,255,255,111,255,255,255,119,32,32
140 DATA 147,32,32,255,255,255,63,34,52,111,255,255,255,33,32
150 DATA 147,32,32,35,47,47,33,32,32,32,43,47,33,32,32
```

Figure 4.4 shows the display produced by this program.

The problem of the limited resolution can be tackled in a number of ways. A simple answer is to stand further away from the BBC Microcomputer's screen so that the lack of fine detail in mode 7 is less obvious — but you can attack the problem at its source by using a smaller grid to cover the image. This gives more squares and hence more data for the drawing program. You would have to then change to one of the other graphics modes and perhaps draw the shape point by point.

As mentioned at the beginning of the chapter, the BBC Microcomputer has available a number of methods of displaying information on the screen. The picture of the butterfly has been drawn using the Teletext mode 7 display. For finer detail other graphics modes are available. For example, mode 5 gives a picture made up from 160 points by 256 points.

The screen co-ordinates

Before you can place a character precisely at any position on the screen, you need to be able to specify that position to the BBC Microcomputer. This position has to be specified in terms of its distance as measured from the bottom of the screen and its distance as measured from the left-hand side of the screen. In the graphics modes, each point on the screen is referred to by means of these distances which are called its screen 'co-ordinates'.

Figure 4.4   Butterfly as displayed on the screen.

These distances cannot, of course, be measured in inches or centimetres because if, for example, you wanted to draw a single line from the bottom left-hand corner of the screen to the centre of the screen, you would need the centre of the screen to remain true, whatever the size of the screen. Clearly what is needed is a means of measuring that is independent of the size of the screen. This has been arranged by specifying that the screen is 1280 'units' wide and 1024 'units' high. This number of units remains the same irrespective of the size of the television and the mode and type of graphics display (mode 7 excepted).

Thus a horizontal position can be between 0, for a position on the extreme left-hand side of the screen, and 1280 for a position on the far right. The centre of the screen has a horizontal position 640 units from the left-hand side of the screen.

A vertical position can be between 0, for a position at the bottom of the screen, and 1024 for a position at the top of the screen. The centre of the screen has a vertical position of 512 units from the bottom of the screen.

When the position of any point on the screen is given in terms of its co-ordinates, the two distances have to be written together and in the right order. The first co-ordinate gives the distance of the point from the left-hand side of the screen; the second co-ordinate gives the distance from the bottom of the screen. The co-ordinate of the centre of the screen is therefore specified as 640,512.

Before you can use any of the graphics, you need to choose the resolution (i.e. the amount of detail) you require. The BBC Microcomputer offers a choice from resolutions of 160, 320 or 640 points across the screen, and you make your selection by choosing the mode. You will remember that the mode in which the BBC Microcomputer works when first turned on is 7, and that you used mode 5 earlier in the chapter for writing coloured text. Mode 7 only allows the display of text and some very crude graphics using the Teletext format. It is more exciting to use another mode. The next section looks at mode 5 because it is available on both the Model A and Model B of the BBC Microcomputer. This mode provides 32 lines of 20 characters for text, and 160 spots horizontally for the graphics display. Although this is the lowest resolution available on the BBC Microcomputer, it does allow the use of up to four colours. There are eight display modes numbered 0 to 7. Their complete specifications are given in Chapter 5.

Writing anywhere on the screen

You now have a choice of how to write to the screen. Either you can use the

PRINT instruction to give messages or you can use graphics characters. You then have a further choice in that you can write the graphics and text to the screen independently or you can arrange to print messages at positions controlled by the graphics instructions. This section investigates the latter.

You need two new BASIC terms: VDU 5 and MOVE. VDU 5 is the instruction to the BBC Microcomputer to print any further messages at the position set by any graphics instructions. MOVE defines the graphics position on the screen.

Suppose you want a program to print the following message across the centre of the screen:

HELLO THERE

The complete program is as follows:

```
10 MODE 5
20 VDU 5
30 MOVE 300,500
40 PRINT "HELLO THERE"
```

Screen patterns and colour

The instruction for setting the colour of anything drawn or written using graphics instructions is GCOL 0,X where X represents the colour number, as for text foreground. Thus the four colours available in mode 5 can be set using one of the following:

GCOL 0,0 (to set the graphics to black)
GCOL 0,1 (to set the graphics to red)
GCOL 0,2 (to set the graphics to yellow)
GCOL 0,3 (to set the graphics to white)

A fascinating display can be produced by writing a character to the screen in both random colours and at random positions. It looks rather like stars twinkling. The program is:

```
10 MODE 5
20 VDU 5
30 X=RND(1280)
40 Y=RND(1024)
50 GCOL 0,RND(4)−1
70 MOVE X,Y
```

55

```
80 PRINT "★"
90 GOTO 30
```

You will be interested in another fascinating example of drawing in colour. On Ordnance Survey maps colours represent heights. You can imitate this use of colours in terms of the screen representing the map and colours representing heights. For simplicity, take the height at any point as given by the following formula, where X,Y are the co-ordinates of that point:

height = X★X + Y★Y

Incidentally this gives a low on the bottom left-hand corner of the screen; this will be represented by black. The formula gives highest ground at the top right-hand corner of the screen; this will be represented by white. Since the height is given by a formula, the computer can work out the height at any point in terms of its position across and up the screen. Hence the computer can draw a contour map on the screen by printing in the appropriate colour to represent the different heights of the map. Black can represent the lowest area of the screen; red a medium height contour; yellow a higher one; and white the highest. Thus the characters are printed, row by row, in an appropriate colour, depending on height. A program scheme for generating this contour map is shown below:

```
 10 MODE 5
 20 VDU 5
 30 FOR X=0 TO 1280 STEP 80
 40 FOR Y=0 TO 1024 STEP 40
 50 height= ((★X)+(Y★Y))/2000
 60 IF height<=80 THEN GCOL 0,0
 70 IF height>80 THEN GCOL 0,1
 80 IF height>400 THEN GCOL 0,2
 90 IF height>800 THEN GCOL 0,3
100 MOVE X,Y
110 PRINT "X"
120 NEXT Y
130 NEXT X
```

In this program 'height' is the variable to represent the height on the contour map. The four condition instructions in lines 60 to 90 test the height and assign an appropriate colour. The PRINT instruction prints in the graphics colour according to the VDU 5 instruction. Line 100 causes the graphics position to be set at the position X,Y ready for the following line to print an X. The computation in line 50 gives a value for height.

Attractive alternative contour maps can be produced by using other formulae to compute the height at any point. The following program illustrates one such alternative:

```
10 MODE 5
20 VDU 5
30 FOR X=1 TO 1280 STEP 80
40 FOR Y=1 TO 1024 STEP 40
50 height = INT(X*Y)^(1/3)/30
60 MOVE X,Y
70 GCOL 0, height: PRINT "X"
80 NEXT Y
90 NEXT X
```

Here there are the same four height intervals. The height is now calculated using a more complicated-looking expression at line 50, where the symbol ^ means 'raised to a power'. (Thus ^1/3 means 'the cube root of'.) The instruction INT( ) finds the whole number part of whatever number appears in the bracket which follows it. As an example, take the position with X=100 and Y=200. This gives:

X*Y=20000

The cube root of 20000 is 27.144. This divided by 30 is 0.90 which has a whole number part of 0. So the colour of the symbol written to the screen at this point is black.

A wide variety of patterns can be produced by using this method. In general a distinct pattern results from each different way of computing height. There are many ways other than by dividing a range into intervals. For example, the number in the first place after the decimal point in the computed value can be used to set the colour. The selection of the colours when writing to the screen can affect the appearance of the pattern. If you have a Model B of the BBC Microcomputer, then more colours can be used when writing to the screen, and so a finer division of the contours can be arranged.

User-controlled movement

Now that you have produced still displays, you will want to make them move. The program presented in this section makes it possible for the user to control the movement of a shape on the screen. Besides being fascinating in itself, the program illustrates the techniques used in many games programs.

In many computer games there is a standard method for allowing the user to control the movements of parts of the display. It involves the use of the keys centred around the H key. These indicate the direction of the movement required. Since the G key is situated to the left of H, it is used to indicate that movement to the left is required. Similarly with the other surrounding keys as shown in Figure 4.5.

A simple way of making up the shape to move around the screen is to print three ordinary symbols, close together and under each other: 0 ★ #. They produce an image looking somewhat like a little man. The following lines achieve this:

```
40  MOVE X,Y+30 : PRINT "O"
50  MOVE X,Y : PRINT "★"
60  MOVE X,Y-24 : PRINT "#"
```

The first line prints a capital O as the head of the little man, and it prints it just a little above the screen position given by X,Y. The second line prints what is going to form the body of the little man, which is the ★ sign. The legs of the little man are provided by the # symbol which is printed out just below the X,Y position. Clearly every time this group of three lines is executed, it prints a picture of the little man on the screen at the position X,Y.

You can now write a program to allow this little man to be moved around anywhere on the screen you choose, by pressing the appropriate keys centred around the H key. The program should print the man to the screen at continually different places. The following is the complete program:

```
10  X=100 : Y=100
20  MODE 5
30  VDU 5
40  MOVE X,Y+30 : PRINT "O"
50  MOVE X,Y : PRINT "★"
```

Figure 4.5 Control keys and directions.

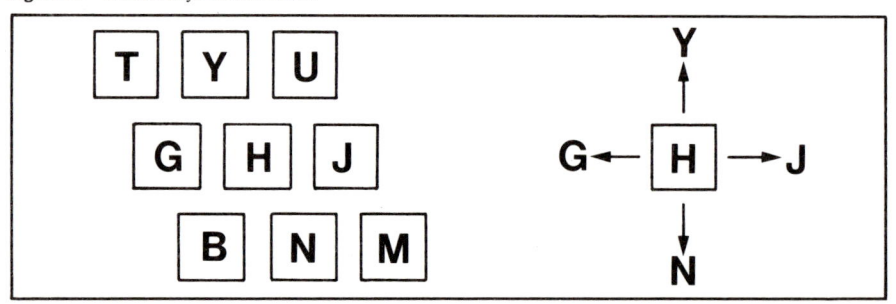

```
 60 MOVE X,Y-24 : PRINT "#"
 70 A$ = INKEY$(10)
 80 IF A$ = " " THEN 70
 90 IF A$ = "Y" THEN Y = Y+10
100 IF A$ = "N" THEN Y = Y-10
110 IF A$ = "G" THEN X = X-10
120 IF A$ = "J" THEN X = X+10
130 GOTO 20
```

Line 20 sets up the graphics mode and also clears the screen as a means of rubbing out the old display before writing a new one. Lines 90 to 120 allow the user to move the little man around on the screen by touching the Y key for 'up', the N key for 'down', the G key for 'left' and the J key for 'right'.

The program does not check to see whether or not the man has moved off the screen. So if the user keeps the man moving in any one direction for too long, he will disappear from view. The user will have to remember which way he went off the screen before being able to use the control keys to bring him back on again.

Animation

Displaying a series of still pictures at a sufficiently rapid rate produces the illusion of continuous movement. This is called 'animation'. All moving picture systems, including films and television, use this effect which relies on the persistence of human vision. The major problem in achieving realistic animation is to generate the successive pictures sufficiently rapidly.

This section gives a program which produces animation of a butterfly flying. The successive frames catch different positions of the butterfly's wings when it is in flight. Figure 4.6 shows the sequence in which the frames are derived.

The first frame with the wings fully extended is the image produced by the program earlier in the chapter. The other frames are obtained in the same way as this one was. In the program the codes for the three frames are read in, and then the frames are plotted repetitively in the sequence one, two, three, two, etc.

The flowchart of the program is given in Figure 4.7, and the program is as follows:

```
10 CLS
20 P=0 : M=1
30 IF P+M <1 OR P+M >3 THEN M=-M
40 P=P+M
50 RESTORE(70+(P★70))
```

```
 60 FOR R=1 TO 6
 70 S=32076+R*40
 80 FOR C=1 TO 15
 90 READ A
100 ?(S+C)=A
110 NEXT C
120 NEXT R
130 GOTO 30
140 DATA
    147,120,124,112,32,32,41,48,224,38,32,224,112,124,116
150 DATA
    147,107,255,255,255,125,48,104,52,224,126,255,255,255,33
160 DATA
    147,32,255,255,255,255,255,126,125,255,255,255,255,53,32
170 DATA
    147,32,34,123,255,255,255,255,111,255,255,255,119,32,32
180 DATA 147,32,32,255,255,255,63,34,52,111,255,255,255,32,32
190 DATA 147,32,32,35,47,47,33,32,32,32,43,47,33,32,32
200 REM P=2
210 DATA 147,32,224,255,124,48,41,48,224,38,224,124,255,52,32
220 DATA
    147,32,34,255,255,255,120,104,52,120,255,255,255,32,32
230 DATA
    147,32,32,111,255,255,255,255,255,255,255,255,63,32,32
240 DATA
    147,32,32,34,255,255,255,255,111,255,255,125,32,32,32
250 DATA 147,32,32,106,255,255,63,34,52,111,255,255,52,32,32
260 DATA 147,32,32,32,47,47,32,32,32,32,43,47,32,32,32
270 REM P=2
280 DATA 147,32,32,32,255,116,41,48,224,38,224,126,53,32,32
290 DATA 147,32,32,32,106,255,126,104,52,120,255,255,33,32,32
300 DATA
    147,32,32,32,106,255,255,255,125,255,255,255,32,32,32
310 DATA 147,32,32,32,42,255,255,255,111,255,255,51,32,32,32
320 DATA 147,32,32,32,104,255,255,34,52,111,255,125,32,32,32
330 DATA 147,32,32,32,110,255,39,32,32,32,43,63,32,32,32
```

Although this program shows how animation can be achieved, it does not work quickly enough to give the illusion of continuous movement. There are several methods of speeding up the plotting of the framed sequence. For instance, it is quicker to plot the changes necessary to convert one frame to the next, rather than to plot the entire frame each time.

Figure 4.6 Frames 1, 2 and 3 for flying Butterfly.

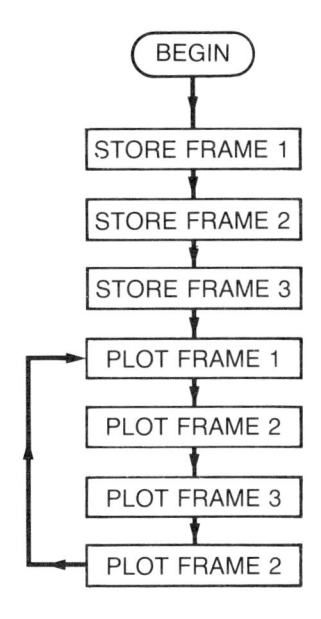

Figure 4.7 Flow chart for mobile display program.

Dynamic simulation

The next program provides a dynamic simulation of a situation which experiences random growth and decay. The display can be taken as the

61

simulation of the growth of a town or of a community of insects. It could also represent the growth of a colony of bacteria. Then it would display a colony that grows initially from a single cell. When it reaches a certain size, it decays to a lower level and then fluctuates between these two levels. A random element in the growth is provided by the RND instruction. A figure at the top left of the screen gives the size of the community by showing the number of cells in it. The program is:

```
 10 MODE 5
 20 VDU 5
 30 I = 10
 40 X = 600: Y = 500
 50 MOVE X,Y:PRINT CHR$(224)
 60 GCOL 0,0
 70 MOVE 250,1000:PRINT CHR$(224);CHR$(224);CHR$(224)
 80 GCOL 0,3
 90 MOVE 0,1000:PRINT "GEN.";I
100 IF I >100 THEN 220
110 A = RND(3) − 2: B = RND(3) − 2
120 IF A = 0 AND B = 0 THEN 110
130 A = A*60: B = B * 40
140 X = X+A: Y = Y+B:
150 IF POINT (X,Y)=0 THEN MOVE X,Y:PRINT CHR$(224): I = I+1
160 IF POINT (X,Y) = −1 THEN X=X−A:Y=Y−B
170 GOTO 60
180 MOVE 250,1000:PRINT CHR$(224);CHR$(224);CHR$(224)
190 GCOL 0,3
200 MOVE 0,1000:PRINT "GEN.";I
210 IF I <70 THEN 110
220 A = (RND(3) −2)*60:B=(RND(3)−2)*40
230 IF A=0 AND B=0 THEN 220
240 X = X+A:Y=Y+B
250 GCOL 0,0
260 IF POINT (X,Y)<>0 THEN MOVE X,Y:PRINT CHR$(224):I=I−1
270 IF POINT (X,Y)=−1 THEN X=X−A:Y=Y−B
280 GOTO 180
```

Drawing lines on the screen

The BBC Microcomputer has a very simple instruction to allow you to draw lines on the screen. DRAW X,Y will draw a line to the point X,Y. Each time you issue this instruction, a new line will be drawn from wherever the previous graphics instruction finished to wherever the current one represents. If you repeat the same DRAW instruction with different values of X and Y, the result will be a new line joining on to the previous one. For instance, the following lines of program will draw a box on the screen:

```
10 MODE 5
20 MOVE 100,100
30 DRAW 100,500
40 DRAW 500,500
50 DRAW 500,100
60 DRAW 100,100
```

The lines could be drawn in, say, red by inserting GCOL 0,1.

You can easily fill in an area with colour by drawing a group of lines together. The following program will set the screen to a red background and then draw in a yellow box just below the centre.

```
10 MODE 5
20 COLOUR 129
30 CLS
40 GCOL 0,2
50 FOR X=400 TO 600 STEP 8
60 MOVE X,300 : DRAW X,500
70 NEXT X
```

Line 20 sets the background colour to red, and line 30 clears the screen to the background colour, thus setting it to red. Line 60 fills in a rectangular area as it repeatedly draws lines from Y=300 to Y=500.

Some pretty patterns can be produced with the line-drawing instruction, especially if it is fed with random positions for drawing to and with randomly coloured lines. The following simple program illustrates this:

```
10 MODE 5
20 GCOL 0,RND(4)-1
30 X=RND(1280)
40 Y=RND(1024)
50 DRAW X,Y
60 GOTO 20
```

Line 10 sets the particular type of graphics. Line 20 generates random colours for the lines. Lines 30 and 40 generate random numbers for the position on the screen for later DRAW instructions. Line 50 draws the lines to the position given by X,Y. Each time the program executes round one loop, one new straight line gets drawn.

Summary

The BBC Microcomputer is particularly renowned for the coloured display that it can produce. Different modes offer different types of graphics.

The BBC Microcomputer can write text in a variety of sizes and colours, both foreground and background. It can also produce coloured pictures. A simple way is by using graphics symbols in the Teletext mode, although there are facilities for finer resolution drawing, using lines of different colours.

The user can program his own characters and move them under his own control, and animation is also possible, but rather slow.

Chapter 5
Special features of the BBC Microcomputer

This chapter collects together information about the BBC Microcomputer. It is not intended to be an exhaustive collection of information. Other books can provide that — but it does include the main points that are of interest to someone starting to use the BBC Microcomputer and wanting an appreciation of its main features. The chapter starts with the specifications of the BBC Microcomputer. It goes on to give a brief introduction to the computer's internal working parts, and finally it discusses some of the BBC Microcomputer's special features.

Specification of the BBC Microcomputer

Manufacturer: Acorn Ltd., Cambridge, England
Microprocessor: 6502
Screen format: Mode 7: 25 rows of 40 characters, Teletext display
    Mode 6: 25 rows of 40 characters, two colour text
    Mode 5: 32 rows of 20 characters, four colour display; also 160 by 256 graphics
    Mode 4: 32 rows of 40 characters, two colour display; also 320 by 256 graphics
    Mode 3: 25 rows of 80 characters, two colour text
    Mode 2: 32 rows of 20 characters, sixteen colour display; also 160 by 256 graphics
    Mode 1: 32 lines of 40 characters, four colour display; also 320 by 256 graphics
    Mode 0: 32 lines of 80 characters, two colour display; also 640 by 256 graphics
The colour numbers: two colour mode
    0 = black
    1 = white
    four colour mode

0 = black
1 = red
2 = yellow
3 = white
sixteen colour mode
0 = black
1 = red
2 = green
3 = yellow
4 = blue
5 = magenta
6 = cyan
7 = white
8 = flashing black/white
9 = flashing red/cyan
10 = flashing green/magenta
11 = flashing yellow/blue
12 = flashing blue/yellow
13 = flashing magenta/green
14 = flashing cyan/red
15 = flashing white/black

Keyboard:	74 keys with letters and numbers laid out in typewriter style
Memory size:	Model A: 16K RAM plus 32K ROM
	Model B: 32K RAM plus 32K ROM
Languages:	When switched on, BASIC is available. Other languages will shortly be available, including PASCAL and FORTH. Assembler language for the 6502 is available from within BASIC.
Graphics repertoire:	Graphics characters are available only in mode 7 (the mode in which the computer is when first turned on). In this mode the display is Teletext-compatible which means that CHR$(147) must proceed any graphics characters on any one line. In the other modes, however, the screen will supply up to 640 point positions across the screen by 256 point positions up the screen, each of which can be individually addressed. The number of points available on the Model A is limited to 320 by 256.
Peripherals:	Model A will connect to a normal colour television, and a cassette recorder. Model B will

Expansion: connect to either an ordinary television or a video monitor. It has a connection for an analogue input to be used with paddles for games programs. It also has connectors for a printer and it has an input/output port available for connection of other electrical gadgetry such as a graph plotter or a bar-code-reader. With extension, Model B can be connected to a floppy disk system and other peripherals such as a lightpen or a speech chip, etc.

It is planned that the BBC Microcomputer should have the possibility of expansion by attaching a further 64K of RAM memory together with either a further 6502 microprocessor or a Z80 microprocessor. The Z80 microprocessor, if used together with a disk system, will allow the BBC Microcomputer to be used with CP/M software which will then make a wide range of programs and languages available for use on the computer. People are working on a wide range of software for both Model A and Model B including a word-processing package.

Programs: Soon after the BBC Microcomputer was launched, advertisements started to appear for programs for it. The number of programs available will no doubt increase dramatically. If floppy disks and a Z80 are attached, an extremely wide range of already written software will be available for the machine. It is anticipated that a wide range of software houses will be writing software packages, including business packages, specially for this microcomputer.

Inside the BBC Microcomputer

Figure 5.1 shows an inside view displaying the various parts that make up the BBC Microcomputer. The screen for the display has to be provided by the user. It could be his own domestic television, or it could be a separate monitor. The keyboard is similar to that of a typewriter, differing only in that it has a few extra keys. Since these external features are familiar, most of this section is devoted to the inside of the computer.

Inside the BBC Microcomputer are the electronics for producing the specialised screen displays, the sound producing circuits, the memory, and of course all the logic for running a sophisticated computer. All of this is mounted on one medium-sized printed circuit board.

A printed circuit board is the most convenient way to mount and interconnect the large number of components of the computer. It has copper tracks laid down on it to connect the mounts into which the various chips are inserted. The layout of the printed circuit board reveals the essential structure of the microcomputer but is not visible, as it is on the underside of the board. Mounted on the printed circuit board are the microprocessor itself, the clock and various other chips.

The power supply unit is mounted in its own separate box inside the main case. It converts the 240 volt alternating supply from the mains to the steady 5 volts and 12 volts needed by the computer components.

The memory available to the user, particularly for storing BASIC programs, is provided by 'random access' chips or RAMS. The information stored in this type of memory can be accessed and can be replaced when required by the program. When the computer is switched off, all the information stored in RAM is lost.

There are of course certain features of the BBC Microcomputer which are always required and which must not be replaced or lost when the computer is turned off. To give just two examples: BASIC must always be available, and the characters to be displayed on the screen should be able to be generated at any time. Such functions are provided by chips with information permanently stored in them. The chips are known as 'read only memories' or ROMS. The positions of the BASIC and the operating system ROMs are shown in Figure 5.1.

The sockets for connecting the BBC Microcomputer to other devices are at the edge of the printed circuit board and at the back of the case. The empty mouldings and spaces on the printed circuit board permit the expansion of the computer. Extra facilities such as the Econet interface and the disk interface can be fitted by inserting the appropriate components and chips in the empty spaces.

Special features

The BBC Microcomputer's clock
The BBC Microcomputer has a very accurate built-in clock which can be accessed from a BASIC program. The time on the clock can be obtained

by using TIME. The following instruction gives a number which is the number of centiseconds since the computer was turned on (a centisecond is one hundredth of a second):

PRINT TIME

Thus if the instruction produces the result 2000, it is 2000 centiseconds (which is 2000/100 or 20 seconds) since the computer was switched on.

To convert TIME to a twelve-hour clock, you can use the following few lines of program:

```
10 SEC = (TIME DIV 100)MOD 60
20 MIN = (TIME DIV 6000)MOD 60
30 HOUR = (TIME DIV 360000) MOD 12
```

If the execution of these lines is followed by:

PRINT "The time is ";HOUR;" ";MIN;" ";SEC

Figure 5.1 Inside view of the BBC Microcomputer.

there will be a printout of the form:

The time is 2 24 32

This indicates that it is twenty four minutes and thirty two seconds past two hours after the computer was turned on.

It is possible for a program to reset TIME back to zero on any occasion when it is convenient to do so. Hence TIME is called a 'pseudo' variable. An expression of the following form will reset the value held by the variable TIME back to zero:

TIME = 0

If you now cause the program to print out the value of TIME, it will give the time in centiseconds since the value for TIME was reset to zero. The clock may be used when precise timing is required in a program for a sequence of activities, or to generate delays. For example, a simple program to make the BBC Microcomputer act as an egg timer could be as follows:

```
10 PRINT "Enter the number of minutes delay required"
20 INPUT mins
30 TIME = 0
40 IF TIME < mins * 60 * 100 THEN 40
50 REM SOUND OUTPUT
60 FOR S = 1 TO 1000
70 SOUND S MOD 3, - 15, S * S, 1
80 NEXT S
```

See the section on sound later in this chapter for more details of the SOUND instruction.

The program cycles on line 40 until the given time when it commences the alarm routine.

Available storage

When the BBC Microcomputer is switched on, it always displays the amount of RAM memory available to you. Model A shows 16K and Model B shows 32K.

Your BASIC program starts, not at the lowest position in memory, but at 4K up in memory. The first 4K or so is used as a working area by the computer itself and is not available for storing BASIC programs. The screen also takes up some of the memory — the amount depends on the mode. When the BBC Microcomputer is first turned on, the display will automatically be in mode 7 which takes up 1K of memory. The memory used by the screen is always at the highest possible location. For Model A of the BBC Microcomputer, using mode 7, 4K of its 16K of RAM is used by the computer for its own internal operation, and 1K is used for the screen. This leaves 11K for your program. In mode 5, which you have used for some of the animated displays, the amount of memory required just for the screen is 10K. With the 4K needed for internal operation, a program using this mode must be no longer than 2K. Modes 0,1,2 and 3 take 16K, or more, of memory just for the screen display. So these modes cannot be used with a Model A because there is not enough memory there.

Examining and altering the contents of a memory location

The BBC Microcomputer uses a question mark followed by a number to represent a memory location. For example, the following represents memory location 5000:

?5000

If you want to examine the contents of memory location 5000, then the following simple instruction will print out the contents of this location for you.

PRINT?5000

(This is unlike most computers which look at the contents of a memory location using an instruction called PEEK.)

If you want to alter the number that is stored in this memory location to, say, the value 3, then you would type and enter:

?5000=3

If you now type and enter the following, you will get the number 3 because this is the number that you put there.

PRINT?5000

When using this sort of instruction for altering the contents of memory locations, do remember first of all that any one memory location can only hold a number between 0 and 255. Also bear in mind that the computer uses for its own purposes all memory locations up to 3584. If you try altering any of these, you may get some very funny effects. If this happens, press the BREAK key — but you may well lose your program in the process.

How the BBC Microcomputer stores a program

A BASIC program is stored in the BBC Microcomputer starting at location 3584. It is stored as a simple list of program lines as illustrated in

Figure 5.2. Each character and BASIC word is represented by a code. Each line of a BASIC program is stored character by character with BASIC words represented by one individual code. For example, a word such as PRINT is reduced to the single code 241. The start of each line is marked by the code 13, followed by two bytes representing the BASIC line number. This is then followed by a count of the number of characters in

Figure 5.2 How a BASIC program is stored.

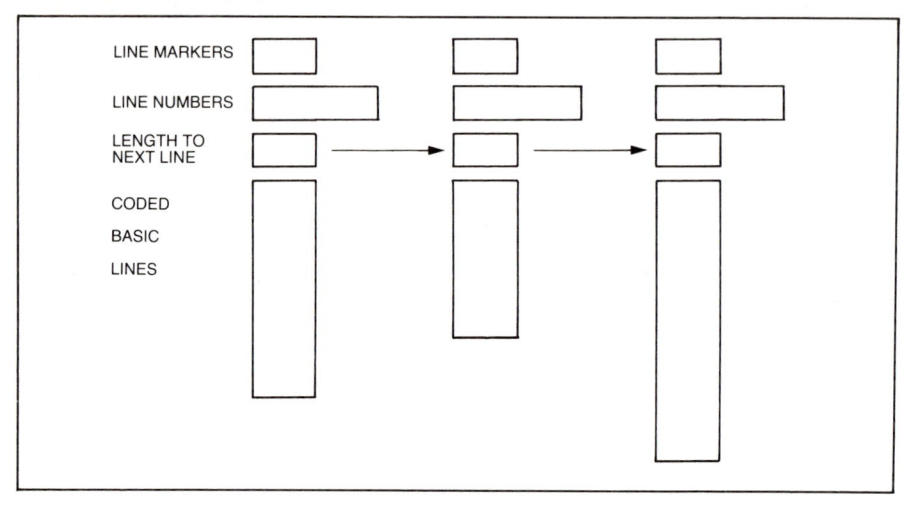

TABLE 5.1

Location number	code	Character or BASIC word
3584	13	start of line
3585	0	line number
3586	10	line number
3587	8	length of this line (to next line length code)
3588	32	space
3589	80	P
3590	61	=
3591	49	1
3592	13	start of line
3593	0	line number
3594	20	line number
3595	10	length of this line (to next line length code)
3596	32	space
3597	81	Q
3598	61	=
3599	80	P
3660	43	+
3601	50	2
3602	13	start of line
3603	0	line number
3604	30	line number
3605	10	length of this line (to next line length code)
3606	32	space
3607	241	PRINT
3608	32	space
3609	80	P
3610	44	,
3611	81	Q
3612	13	start of line
3613	255	end of program

72

the BASIC line. The end of the program is indicated by the code 255, following the code 13 marking a new line.

As an illustration, the following short BASIC program

10 P=1
20 Q=P+2
30 PRINT P,Q

is stored in memory as shown in Table 5.1:

The form of this BASIC program, when stored, is illustrated in Figure 5.3.

You can inspect the codes for the characters and BASIC words. The following instruction allows you to examine the address location 3594 in the area where the program is stored:

PRINT ?3594

Programs are stored in this way to facilitate the procedures by which the BBC Microcomputer operates, including the way in which it stores program lines in correct order, regardless of the order in which they are entered.

Figure 5.3 Storage of a short BASIC program.

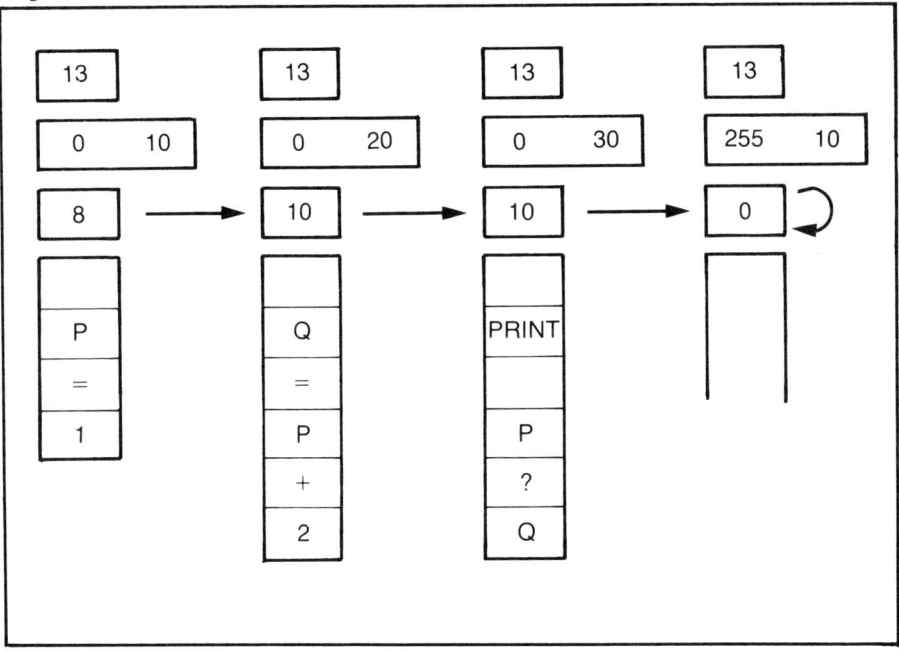

General utilisation of memory

Figure 5.4 shows the way in which the memory within the computer is used for storing both the BASIC program and the operating system. It shows what is called the 'memory map' for the system. You will see that half of the memory is occupied by the ROMs which hold the BASIC and operating system. The memory for the screen resides at the top of the available RAM. For Model B, this is from address 32768 downwards and for Model A, from address 16384 downwards.

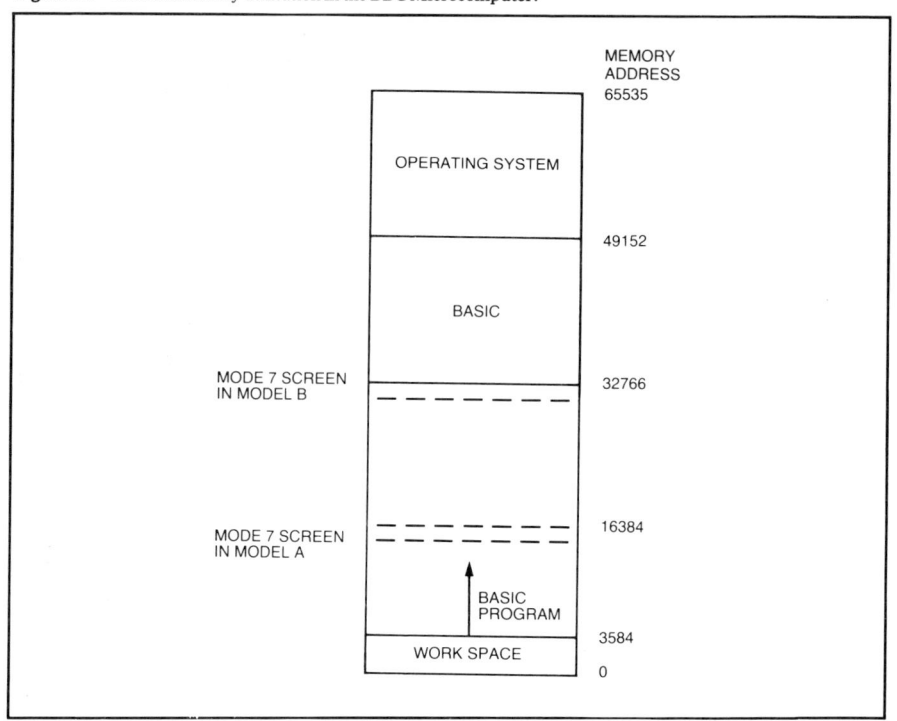

Figure 5.4 General memory utilisation in the BBC Microcomputer.

```
                                              MEMORY
                                              ADDRESS
                                              65535
                    ┌─────────────────────┐
                    │                     │
                    │  OPERATING SYSTEM   │
                    │                     │
                    │                     │
                    ├─────────────────────┤  49152
                    │                     │
                    │                     │
                    │        BASIC        │
                    │                     │
   MODE 7 SCREEN    │                     │  32766
   IN MODEL B       ├ ─ ─ ─ ─ ─ ─ ─ ─ ─ ─ ┤
                    │                     │
                    │                     │
                    │                     │
                    │                     │
   MODE 7 SCREEN    ├ ─ ─ ─ ─ ─ ─ ─ ─ ─ ─ ┤  16384
   IN MODEL A       │         ▲           │
                    │      BASIC          │
                    │     PROGRAM         │
                    ├─────────────────────┤  3584
                    │     WORK SPACE      │
                    └─────────────────────┘  0
```

Sound on the BBC Microcomputer

You will probably have already noticed that there is a little grill on the left-hand side of the keyboard. What you may not realise is that a small loudspeaker is underneath this grill. It is this which produces the small beep-like noise when the BBC Microcomputer is switched on.

You can program the BBC Microcomputer to produce sounds with a wide variety of pitches. Notes can be combined and played together to produce some very pleasing music.

Any musical tune is made up of a series of notes played one after the other. Instruments like the flute or the piccolo can only play one note at a time, while an instrument like a piano can play a number of notes at a time. Each instrument can play notes with a wide variety of different pitches, i.e. some notes sound high and some low. The notes can last for a short time or a long time, can also be loud or soft. You can program all of these aspects of playing a tune with the BBC Microcomputer.

In the BBC Microcomputer there is a special sound-producing chip. This chip will produce up to four independent sounds. Three of them are pure notes, whereas the fourth is more of a noise. This book will concentrate on producing the pure notes.

You will start by programming one note at a time. This means that you will be imitating single notes on an instrument like a flute rather than chords on a piano. You need an instruction of the following form, where each of the four variables C,A,P and D must have values:

SOUND C,A,P,D

C represents the channel and this specifies which part of the sound generator chip is to be used to produce the tone. As there are three channels which produce a pure note, you can give C a value of one, two or three for a pure note. If C has the value four, then you will get the noise.

A affects the loudness of the note. It may be a number between zero and minus fifteen. Zero represents no sound, just as if the note were turned off — and is a value you are not likely to use. Minus fifteen produces the loudest note, while a number between zero and minus fifteen produces a correspondingly increasing loudness. Minus seven, for instance, will be quieter than minus fifteen. If you listen to a series of notes of different loudness, going between zero and minus fifteen, you will actually hear what seems like the biggest change between zero and minus seven. From there on, you will only hear what appears to be slightly smaller changes.

P represents the pitch of the note. In musical terms pitch on the BBC Microcomputer may be specified in quarter semitones where a pitch of fifty-two gives the note middle C on the musical scale. Each time you increase P by one, you increase the pitch of the note by one quarter semitone. Thus E, which is two tones above middle C, is sixteen quarter semitones up. The maximum value of P is two hundred and fifty-five.

D determines how long the note lasts. It gives the duration in twentieths of a second. So to produce a note lasting for half a second would require a duration of ten, i.e. ten-twentieths of a second.

The following are three lines of program to produce three notes, the A below middle C, the B below middle C and middle C:

```
10 SOUND 1,-15,40,10
20 SOUND 1,-15,48,10
30 SOUND 1,-15,52,10
```

All these three notes get produced one after another on the same channel. So you have the rather odd phenomenon that the program will stop running before the notes stop coming out of the computer. The computer will remember up to four notes per channel and play them in order. If you send notes to any of the other channels, these channels will act independently. If you want notes to sound together, i.e. chords, they have to come out from the various channels at the same time. To some extent it is not advisable to play chords because, whereas the chords as played on musical instruments produce pleasing effects, on the BBC Microcomputer, they may sound discordant. This is due to the manufacturers of the BBC Microcomputer having had to make some compromise when programming the sound chip. So although individual notes sound fairly true, notes sounded together may clash to some extent.

You may like to experiment with producing noise on the fourth channel. Do realise, though, that the noise that channel four produces is affected to some extent by the note that channel one is playing.

Games programs can be very much improved by having some sort of sound output. For example sometimes it is useful to have a beep every time a key is pressed, so as to acknowledge that the computer has received an instruction. Also, say, if you have a ball bouncing around on the screen, you can get a nice sort of realism by programming a sound every time it bounces off the edge of the screen or off an obstacle like a bat.

Conclusions

This book has aimed to provide an easy introduction to using the BBC Microcomputer, and it has described many applications in which the BBC Microcomputer can be used to good effect simply by loading and running a program. There are a large number of applications of this kind including business applications which require no knowledge of how the BBC Microcomputer works and need only a minimal knowledge of the instructions required to operate it. In these circumstances the program is all important. The BBC Microcomputer is merely a vehicle for running the program. A special purpose system of this kind can demonstrate its worth by paying for itself in quite a short time. However the BBC Microcomputer is extremely versatile, being capable of as many activities as it can be programmed for. This versatility can be harnessed by running different programs for each of a range of applications.

Purchased programs do not always do exactly what the user requires so that it is useful to be able to program the BBC Microcomputer in order to modify programs. Whether for this reason or as a result of inquisitiveness about how to tap the full potential of the BBC Microcomputer, it is useful to be able to write programs. An introduction to programming the BBC Microcomputer is provided by this book, but it is only an introduction, and Appendix 1 indicates several sources of information which can be used for further study.

The importance of the BBC Microcomputer when used as an educational tool has been stressed more than once in these pages. Its importance as an example of modern technology should not be overlooked. It has a merit merely in existing as an available product of the technology that will be used increasingly in the future, by providing an appreciation of how the technology is applied in everyday situations.

When viewed from different perspectives, the BBC Microcomputer is seen as a tool which can be used in a number of ways. This book has attempted to introduce many of these uses and also to indicate the sources of information which will help in developing these avenues further.

Appendix 1

Further reading

This appendix gives some books and magazines which are suitable for further reading to follow up particular topics that are mentioned, introduced or developed in this book.

Useful books for programming on the BBC Microcomputer

1. *BASIC Programming on the BBC Microcomputer* by Neil Cryer and Pat Cryer (Prentice Hall, 1982).
This book starts from first principles and goes on to give a comprehensive treatment of programming in BASIC for the BBC Microcomputer. It explains how to use the facilities of the BBC Microcomputer for BASIC programming, and should be an invaluable reference book.

2. *BBC Microcomputer System User Guide*
This book comes free with the BBC Microcomputer and provides a comprehensive definition of the instructions within BBC BASIC, together with guidance on how to connect the computer up and attach various peripherals. This is not a book on BASIC programming.

3. *The Personal Computer Book* by R. Bradbeer (Input Two-nine, 1980).
This is a highly regarded general introduction to microcomputers.

Magazines

4. Computing Today
5. Personal Computer World
6. Practical Computing
7. Computer and Video Games

These are perhaps the major four of the popular computing magazines — although there are several others, and new ones come out frequently. These four cover the whole field of computing. They publish listings of programs, comments on computers and their uses, general articles on computing and introductions to computing, and addresses of local clubs, etc. They have all given the BBC Microcomputer considerable attention.

Appendix 2

Glossary

Array
A block of sequential segments of memory reserved by, for example, DIM A$(20). They are named, in this case, A$(1), A$(2) . . . A$(20) giving a set of names which can be used in the same way as ordinary variable names, but with the convenience that they include a bracketed index.

BASIC
The computer language available when the BBC Microcomputer is turned on, and in which commands to it are expressed. BASIC actually stands for Beginner's All-purpose Symbolic Instruction Code.

Byte
A memory location. Its contents can be any one of 256 possibilities.

Chip
Literally, the chip of silicon from which an integrated circuit is fabricated, but used popularly to refer to the integrated circuit itself.

Cursor
The flashing bar on the BBC Microcomputer's screen which indicates the position at which the next item will be displayed.

Database
An organised collection of data from which either data or the properties of items of data can easily be retrieved.

Disk
A disk on which programs or data can be stored as magnetic patterns on the surface of the disk, and from which recorded information can be rapidly retrieved. Also known as a floppy disk.

DOS
Disk Operating System. A program to facilitate the storage of information on disk and its retrieval from the disk.

Flow chart
A diagram indicating in stylised form the steps of a computation. It is used as an aid in developing programs.

Graphics
Pictures produced by a computer.

Integrated circuit
An electronic circuit fabricated in extreme miniature form on a silicon chip typically a few millimetres square.

K
1K stands for 1 kilobyte of memory, and gives the size of a memory consisting of 1024 storage locations.

Machine code
The code in which instructions must be conveyed to a microprocessor in order that it may respond to them directly.

Microprocessor
Physically, a very complex integrated circuit. Functionally, an electronic device that can be programmed and can, in consequence, perform a variety of tasks.

Peripheral
Equipment that can be attached to the BBC Microcomputer, and can be used in conjunction with it because the latter can control it. Examples are cassette units and printers.

Printed circuit board
A board on which conducting connections and sockets are mounted so that it can support and interconnect electronic components and integrated circuits.

Program
An ordered sequence of commands given to the BBC Microcomputer, so that when it obeys them it automatically performs a specified task.

RAM
Random-access memory. Memory whose contents are lost when the power supply is turned off. The amount of RAM determines how much memory is available for the user to store programs and data.

RETURN
When the RETURN key is pressed at the end of a line, that line is sent to the BBC Microcomputer to be dealt with. For example, commands are

then executed, and program lines are stored.

ROM
Read-only memory. This is permanent memory, typically used to store information that is always required, such as that which provides BASIC. This memory is not available to store the user's programs: it provides facilities required by the user.

Software
Software means programs, although it includes utility programs as well as the user's own programs. This contrasts with hardware, which refers to the physical equipment of a computing system.

User port
One of the connections at the rear of the BBC Microcomputer, which can be used to send or receive signals under the control of the user's program.

Word processor
A system for processing textual material electronically and then printing it or, perhaps, transmitting it to a similar system. In this context, the processing is mainly editing.

Index

animation 37, (57), 59
array 37-8

background 45-7
BASIC 19, 80
break key 15
butterfly
  drawing 51-3
  animation 59-61
byte 13, 80

caps lock 14, 15
CAT 40
Ceefax 45, 51
channel 75
character 14
chord 75, 76
CHR$ 41
clock 68-9
CLS 26, 29, 36
COLOUR 45-8
colour 45-57
  background 45-7
  foreground 45-7, 55
  numbers 65
coloured pictures 47
coloured writing 45
coordinates 53
copy key 18, 27
cursor 14, 80
cursor control key 18, 27

DATA 52, 60
decisions 30
delete key 18, 27
DIM 37
DRAW 62
drawing 51
  a butterfly 51
  lines 62
  patterns 57

dynamic simulation 61

editing 18
ELSE 31
error messages 21
escape key 15, 40
expansion, of computer 67

FOR 34
foreground colour
  see colour, foreground

GCOL 56
GOTO 32, 34
graphics 2, 47, 65

IF 30
INPUT 29

key,
  arithmetic operation 22
  break 15
  caps lock 14, 15
  copy 18
  cursor control 18, 27
  delete 18, 27
  escape 15
  return 15
  shift lock 14, 15
keyboard 14, 66
kilobyte 13, 80

languages 66
  BASIC 5, 19
LEFT$ 21
LEN 20
lines, drawing 62
LIST 27, 28

83

LOAD 16
loading a program 16
loudness 75

memory 13, 48, 66, 74
  examining 71
  location, altering 71
  map 74
  random access 68
  read only 68
  size 66
memory-mapped screen 48
MID$ 35
MODE 45
mode 45, 65
MOVE 55
movement 58

NEXT 34
NEW 27, 28
not equal to 30
number
  colour 65-6
  random 47

OLD 28
Oracle 45, 51

pattern-generating program 47
patterns 57
peripherals 7, 66, 81
pictures, coloured 47
pitch 75
power supply 68
PRINT 20
printed circuit board 68, 81
printer 8, 41
program 67
  decisions in 30
  for an egg timer 70
  loading 16
  line number 25
  pattern-generating 47
  running 25
  saving 39
  storing 71

to translate 37
verifying 40
writing 25
pseudo variable 70

RAM 68
random access memory 68
random number generator 47
READ 52
read only memory 68
resolution 52
RIGHT$ 21
RND 47
ROM 68
RUN 16, 27
running a program 25

SAVE 39
saving programs 39
screen 14, 48
  coordinates 53
  editing facilities 2
  format 65
  movement on 59
  positions 48
scrolling 14
shift lock key 14, 15
simulation, dynamic 61
SOUND 75
sound
  chord 76
  duration 75
  loudness 75
  pitch 75
specifications 65
storage 70
storing programs 71
string 19
switching on 13

Teletext 45, 51
THEN 30
TIME 69
translation program 37-8

user controlled movement 57

variable, pseudo 70
VDU 56
verifying programs 40

Welcome tape 6, 16, 23
writing, coloured 45
writing programs 25